Edited by **Valerie Nye** and **Kathy**

True Stories of **Censorship Battles** in America's Libraries

American Library Association
Chicago 2012

Valerie Nye is the library manager at Santa Fe University of Art and Design's Fogelson Library. She previously worked as a library consultant at the New Mexico State Library, where she started researching and presenting trainings on intellectual freedom and banned books. Nye earned her MLIS from the University of Wisconsin–Madison. She has coauthored two guide books with Kathy Barco and one literary research guide with R. Neil Scott titled *Postmarked Milledgeville: A Guide to Flannery O'Connor's Correspondence in Libraries and Archives*. Nye is a trustee on the board of the New Mexico Library Foundation.

Kathy Barco is currently a children's librarian with Albuquerque's public library. She was youth services coordinator at the New Mexico State Library from 2001 to 2006. Barco earned her MLIS from the University of Southern Mississippi. She has contributed to *Thinking Outside the Book: Essays for Innovative Librarians* and wrote the foreword to *Librarians as Community Partners: An Outreach Handbook*. Barco's *READiscover New Mexico: A Tri-Lingual Adventure in Literacy* won a New Mexico Book Award. She is on the board of the New Mexico Library Foundation and received the New Mexico Library Association's Leadership Award in 2006.

Printed in the United States of America

16 15 14 13 12   5 4 3 2 1

ISBNs: 978-0-8389-1130-3 (paper); 978-0-8389-9362-0 (PDF); 978-0-8389-9387-3 (ePUB); 978-0-8389-9388-0 (Mobipocket); 978-0-8389-9389-7 (Kindle). For more information on digital formats, visit the ALA Store at alastore.ala.org and select eEditions.

Library of Congress Cataloging-in-Publication Data
True stories of censorship battles in America's libraries / edited by Valerie Nye and Kathy Barco.
     p. cm.
Includes bibliographical references and index.
ISBN 978-0-8389-1130-3 (alk. paper)
1. Libraries--Censorship--United States. 2. Intellectual freedom--United States. 3. Librarians--Professional ethics--United States. 4. Libraries--United States--Case studies. I. Nye, Valerie, 1971- II. Barco, Kathy, 1946-
Z711.4.T78 2012
025.2'13--dc23
                    2011031913

Desgin and typesetting by Adrianna Sutton using Minion and Gotham typefaces.
♾ This paper meets the requirements of ANSI/NISO Z39.48–1992 (Permanence of Paper).

To Judy Blume

Of all your wonderful characters, I identify most with Davey Wexler in *Tiger Eyes*, probably because much of the action in the book takes place in New Mexico. Davey and I both attended Los Alamos High School, loved to hike in the canyons around Los Alamos, and worked as candy stripers at the Los Alamos Medical Center. Although Davey wasn't in the band like I was, she did end up in a banned book.

    K.B.

To Gretchen Knief

Your brave defense of *The Grapes of Wrath* in the Kern County library in 1939 when it was banned by the library's board inspires my continual interest in intellectual freedom and my support and admiration for librarians who find themselves the lonely defenders of the First Amendment in their communities. "Ideas don't die because a book is forbidden reading."

    V.N.

CONTENTS

Additional material and updates available at
www.librarycensorship.com

FOREWORD

I DIDN'T start my first novel, *Crank,* expecting publication. Writing the semiautobiographical book was, for me, catharsis. However, as I wrote about this straight-A teen with ambitious dreams, who takes a wrong turn and ends up addicted to crystal meth, I realized the story was bigger than my daughter's—and mine. The story belonged to all those who have been touched by this monster drug, or any addiction, really. The book found a publisher easily, and an editor who believed in the power of the tale. Still, I never expected *Crank* to become the word-of-mouth sensation that it did, eventually becoming a *New York Times* best seller. Nor did I ever dream it would catapult me into the upper echelon of today's YA writers. Neither did I ever expect to receive e-mails like this one (reproduced here verbatim):

Dear Ellen,
First I would like to say that I am a 19-year-old girl named Kimber. I read all of your books but I really need to thank you for *Crank* and *Glass.* I read both of them when I was 17 and I thought they were wonderful.

I had lived that life, I did crystal meth when I was 13 after the suicide of my best friend. You're book was the first book I read that had to do with drugs since I had stopped doing them when I was 16, and it was a rather odd experience to step back into that life and see how self destructive I was.

I know that I am two years late in writing this but I had just got done packing my things to go to college and I found your books. So I re-read them, and it is still an odd experience re-entering that world, but I still want to thank you. I know that sometimes life gets hard, people die, and burdens get hard to bear, but you book is a constant reminder that the things that I had experienced while I did meth, I never want to go through again.

Books like yours can save someone's life, even the people who have gone through those issues. Your books have saved me from myself more times than I can think of and even though I never told you before, I felt you should know.

The thing about books that the small group of people who would prefer that no one reads your books is that books give people a chance to try on other lives. They give people a chance to know what comes with doing drugs without having to do drugs.

Thank you, for everything you have done for me and all your readers. You are appreciated.

Love,
Kimber

E-mails. Snail mail. MySpace. Facebook. Twitter. Various other social networking venues. Between them, I receive hundreds of messages every day from my readers. Some simply thank me for my books, or tell me they were never readers until they found my novels. Others credit me with inspiring their own muses (and often they ask for critique or information on how to publish). But many, many are like Kimber's. They thank me for insight into their own addictions, or the addictions of those close to them. They thank me for veering them away from the path to addiction or suicide. They thank me for letting them know they're not alone, they're not crazy, they are okay. They thank me for literally saving their lives.

It's a heady responsibility, one I don't take lightly. I have a relationship with the Creator and believe my family's pain was given meaning by my ability to help others in need, through my words. So when my books are challenged, I feel it's my duty to push back. Fight back if I have to. Because no one person should be allowed to speak for everyone else. Not for their community, their state, their country. No one person has the right to decide what everyone else can or can't read.

Truthfully, I never expected to become a vocal champion for keeping books on bookshelves. But in September 2009, a challenge to my novel *Glass* (the sequel to *Crank*) gave me no other choice. I had donated a school visit to a charity auction, the proceeds of which were to benefit a bookseller who had insurmountable hospital bills. At this point in my career, the day is worth $3,000, plus travel expenses. The librarian who made the winning bid worked at a middle school in Norman, Oklahoma, a suburb of Oklahoma City. The day was set, the travel paid for, and I was on my way.

Except, three days before the planned visit, a parent challenged content in *Glass* (ostensibly because, while scanning the book, she noticed the f-bomb). So, okay, I understand challenges lead to a review process, as this one did. The book was pulled from the middle school bookshelves until there was a resolution. Meanwhile, however, the parent complained that she didn't want her child to see the author (me . . . me!) speak. When informed that there was an opt-out, she said that she didn't want *any* child to see me speak. I don't know who she was, or why she had such power, but the school superintendent agreed. My visit was canceled.

Okay, I said, if you don't want me in the middle school, how about a high school? No. Ellen Hopkins was officially banned from district schools. Sheesh. Without a review, even. Because, as anyone who has seen one of my talks will tell you, the takeaway is how choices teens make can and will affect them for the rest of their lives. That even the best of kids can make a bad decision that will change everything for them. Just like one bad choice did for my beautiful daughter.

Karin Perry, the fabulous middle school librarian, did arrange for me to speak to the community at the Hillsdale Baptist Freewill College. I invited the concerned parent, the superintendent, and the review committee to come listen. Not one of them did. Even so, that might have been the end of it, except that a newsperson from a local television station decided to get involved, offering his "My Two Cents" on-camera op-ed piece. I watched a video clip in which he admitted that he hadn't actually read *Glass,* but "in scanning it" he found the dreaded naughty word. Much too mature for middle school readers, he said, and now that the book was off middle school shelves, the next step was excising it from the high schools.

Okay, now I was pissed. First of all, though the book may be too mature for *some* middle school readers, I can show you letters like Kimber's, telling me they started using drugs at age twelve or thirteen, and some even younger. Or that they experienced childhood sexual abuse, beginning when they were six. Or that they were raped at age ten. These middle school children need books that can help them know they're not alone. They're not crazy. They're okay. By high school, well, if they haven't heard the f-word, they've been raised in a complete vacuum.

I guess I could have been quietly pissed. Instead, I did what any upstanding YA author would do. I organized an e-mail campaign among over 20,000 of my closest MySpace, Facebook, and Twitter friends. Asked them to respectfully (although I suspect many were less than respectful) message both the television station and the superintendent's office, telling them why my books were important to have in their libraries.

After we tied up their servers for a very long time, the newscaster did another opinion piece. *Glass* was, in his opinion, still too mature for middle school readers. But "Ellen Hopkins has a lot of friends," and he had decided that my message was a good one. The book, post-challenge, remains on middle and high school shelves in Norman, Oklahoma, thanks to strong-willed librarians and a fair review committee.

Had that parent understood how famous she was going to make me, she likely would have kept her mouth shut. The story of Ellen Hopkins being banned in Oklahoma got picked up by the Associated Press and was carried in newspapers nationwide. The UK *Guardian* told the story in England. I was in *School Library Journal,* the *Christian Science Monitor,* and even on the *Conservatives for Palin* website. Kid you not. My name and the dreaded S.P., in the same sentence? The irony is luscious.

See, I wrote this poem for Banned Books Week. (More irony, actually. The Norman thing was the same week!) Simon and Schuster produced my "Manifesto" as a broadside and distributed it to booksellers and libraries around the country. The Sarah Palin blogger happened to see a Banned Books Week display featuring "Manifesto," side by side with a story about S.P. questioning a Wasilla librarian about how she would proceed if a book was challenged. The blogger was sooooooooooooooooo offended! Okay, to be fair, the poem talks about "zealots and bigots and false patriots." Just saying.

Here's where the irony goes really wrong. The same month I was banned in Norman, several other authors experienced school visit cancellations and preemptive pulls increased. This was right after President Obama was banned from classrooms, due to potential "brainwashing." His videotaped message: work hard, stay in school, give back. The uber-conservative base was emboldened. In Michigan, a number of supposedly offensive YA books were stripped from shelves and burned in the street. Books. Burned. You see what can happen when one entity decides for everyone?

The year 2010 brought new challenges. In Stockton, Missouri, by a 7–0 vote of the school board, Sherman Alexie's brilliant *The Absolutely True Diary of a Part-Time Indian* was pulled from bookshelves. In another corner of Missouri, a university professor complained about "dirty young adult literature," likening Laurie Halse Anderson's hugely important book, *Speak,* to soft porn. My own book *Identical* was also called pornographic. The two deal with rape and childhood sexual abuse. Sad to think some people might get turned on, reading about such things.

I also had another, even more public "dis-invitation," this time from a Houston-area teen book festival. And this time it was a librarian who initiated the problem, apparently "fearing for the safety" of her middle school students. She enlisted the aid of a couple of parents, who went to the school board. The superintendent, "not wanting controversy," told the organizers to remove me from the roster.

I almost let this one go, except that the superintendent said two things: that he hadn't read my books but rather relied on Internet research (a site that rates content . . . grrrrr); and "There are more authors out there than we could ever have at our festivals." The last remark I took personally (hey, I'm not just "any author"). But the first is all too often the case when it comes to censorship. I organized a boycott by my readers and let the other authors know I'd done so. One by one, five of the seven remaining authors (Pete Hautman, Melissa de la Cruz, Matt de la Pena, Tera Lynn Childs, and Brian Meehl) withdrew, as a unified stand against censorship.

If the superintendent didn't want controversy, it didn't work out so well. This story went even bigger than Norman. In an interview, Hautman talked about "not doing anything" the times he had been uninvited from speaking, and how he later regretted it. De la Cruz blogged about growing up in the Philippines, where a dictator decided what people could and couldn't read. Unfortunately, the festival was canceled. And in the wake of that, my motives were questioned ("she's only out for money/fame/publicity"). I was called "disgusting" and "sick" (for writing about the subjects I do). Those words hurt. But if I've helped keep a spotlight trained on censorship, helped people remember the importance of every reader's right to have access to the book he or she most needs, it was worth every hurtful comment.

Bottom line. No book is right for every reader. So fine. Don't read my books if they offend you or you hate poetry or need a fairy-tale ending. If you don't want your own children to read them, tell them they can't (and see what happens). But don't make that decision without reading them first. Don't scan for offenses. Read in context. You might decide the messages they carry are positive, if strong. You might even find a way to open communication with your kids. Words can't damage them. But ignorance surely can.

Librarians and teachers, and other gatekeepers, please remember that every child's experience is different, and so is their need for reading materials. Recently a young man in small-town Kentucky asked his school librarian for books with gay characters. Because, of course, he is gay and needs to know that he's not alone. Not crazy. That he's okay. The librarian told him such books were "inappropriate." That young man, Brent Taylor, could have skulked away. Instead he went public, and his story appeared in newspapers and online journals from California to New York.

If people like Brent Taylor and Ellen Hopkins and others like us don't stand up to would-be censors, this country will regress. Plenty of people would be happy to see that happen. But books are knowledge. And knowledge is power. And only by empowering future generations will they understand, individually and en masse, that they're not alone. They're not crazy. They're okay.

And here, for those who haven't seen it, is "Manifesto."

Manifesto
To you zealots and bigots and false
patriots who live in fear of discourse.
You screamers and banners and burners
who would force books
off shelves in your brand name
of greater good.
You say you're afraid for children,
innocents ripe for corruption
by perversion or sorcery on the page.
But sticks and stones do break
bones, and ignorance is no armor.
You do not speak for me,
and will not deny my kids magic
in favor of miracles.
You say you're afraid for America,
the red, white and blue corroded
by terrorists, socialists, the sexually
confused. But we are a vast quilt
of patchwork cultures and multi-gendered
identities. You cannot speak for those
whose ancestors braved
different seas.
You say you're afraid for God,
the living word eroded by Muhammed
and Darwin and Magdalene.
But the omnipotent sculptor of heaven
and earth designed intelligence.
Surely you dare not speak
for the father, who opens
his arms to all.
A word to the unwise.
Torch every book.
Char every page.
Burn every word to ash.
Ideas are incombustible.
And therein lies your real fear.

Ellen Hopkins

INTRODUCTION

LOOKING BACK, it seems inevitable that we would produce a book about librarians' experiences with banned books. After all, we've been giving our presentation, Banned Books Exposed, for several years for library staff members, church and community groups, and librarians at state and regional library conferences. Val provides a brief history of banned books and talks about the American Library Association's role in documenting challenges and supporting librarians who are faced with demands for censoring library material. Kathy gives booktalks on several books that have been banned or challenged. The booktalks never call attention to the books' controversial aspects but are designed simply to entice the audience to want to read them. Invariably, people come up to us afterward to confess and tell stories about books that have been saved. The librarians who confess often tell us that they have dealt with a difficult challenge in their library by quietly removing the book from the collection. We are also fortunate to hear fascinating stories of bravery when librarians have vocally protected the inclusion of a controversial book in their communities.

In 2009, Judy Blume was being honored at the University of Southern Mississippi's Fay B. Kaigler Children's Book Festival. Confident that our Banned Books Exposed presentation was a natural fit for the festival, we submitted a proposal and were invited to attend as presenters. Both times we gave our presentation during the three-day event, we heard stories of challenges. It wasn't until we were standing in Judy Blume's incredibly long book-signing queue that an incident—we later realized—became the catalyst for this book.

From our very first presentation to the presentations we give today, we always wear our banned books T-shirts. As we stood in Judy Blume's line, a woman behind us suddenly said, "I was at your presentation yesterday. I own a banned books T-shirt. I wore it to my school once on the first day of Banned Books Week. My principal made me go home and change clothes. I think I might try wearing it again next time Banned Books Week rolls around."

Later that evening, sharing a plate of fried green tomatoes at a Hattiesburg restaurant, we talked about the woman and her banned books T-shirt. Reflecting on some of the tales we had been told, we realized that experiencing a challenge to library materials might be the most frightening professional experience a librarian encounters, especially when he or she is a solo librarian or feels a lack of professional support. We also knew that stories of victories in saving library material, especially in the face of vocal opposition, might lend strength to librarians who initially felt threatened when experiencing a challenge.

From that moment on, we found ourselves on the journey to publication. We knew our first step would be to find a publisher. Aiming high, we submitted a proposal to ALA Editions. We were thrilled to be given the green light, and the real trip began. It turns out we've been en route to writing this book all along; we just hadn't noticed all the road signs. There have been some amazing coincidences and a lot of luck.

Once we signed our ALA contract, we put out the call for submissions. Searching far and wide, we contacted library associations in every state and sought out librarians we read about in the news to see if they would be interested in submitting a story. Even before querying ALA Editions, we knew we would be giving the Banned Books Exposed presentation at the 2010 Mountain Plains Library Association conference in Oklahoma City. We planned to blitz conference goers with information about our book. To that end we designed special business cards, conference bag inserts, and buttons. When we got to the conference, we weren't shy about trying to get folks to jump on our "banned wagon." In the elevator of the hotel: "Hi, I'm Kathy. Have you ever experienced a book challenge?" On the bus to the Western Heritage Museum and Cowboy Hall of Fame: "Hi, I'm Valerie. Has anyone tried to ban a book from your library?"

Being pushy paid off in a big way. We met several people who agreed to submit their stories. Other folks gave us leads to colleagues who might be interested in writing about their experiences. The most exciting suggestion of all came from a "dine-around dinner companion" who described Oklahoma's recent "Ellen Hopkins incident." Before we even returned home from the conference, we knew things had gone more than okay in OK.

The banned wagon picked up speed quickly after that. We were able to recruit Ellen Hopkins to write the foreword. We tracked down the librarian, Karin Perry, at the epicenter of the Hopkins incident, who agreed to tell her story. We had seen Susan Patron, librarian and author of the Newbery-winning *Higher Power of Lucky*, speak at a Mountain Plains Library Association conference in Salt Lake City in 2008. She graciously offered to submit something.

We've received some amazing contributions for this book. It has been an adventure to travel vicariously on the banned wagon as librarians share their experiences with censorship. Not every excursion has a happy ending, but we have found inspiration in every single journey.

We believe these stories contain several recurring themes that can offer strength to librarians before and after a challenge. The most important lesson we hear repeated in these essays is a call for each library to have a collection development policy and a materials reconsideration policy in place before a challenge occurs. The collection development policy describes the community and the material a library will and will not collect. Collection development policies often include the ALA Library Bill of Rights and the Freedom to Read Statement. The materials reconsideration policy provides information about how a complaint about library material will be handled. It outlines the specific responsibilities of the person challenging the library material and the specific responsibilities of the library staff and the library's governing body. These documents are essential and provide the road map for moving forward even against the most precarious roadblocks endured during a difficult public challenge.

Another common theme in these essays is that challenges to library materials occur frequently and in all types of libraries: school, academic, public, and special libraries. These challenges can come from anyone at any time, including people on a library's staff. As several stories in this volume illustrate, perhaps the most common form of censorship—silent censorship—occurs when a librarian decides quietly to withdraw a book from a library's collection. And there are stories of librarians acting even more silently still, when a selector doesn't order a book because it might cause a controversy.

Finally, there is an ongoing theme of brave librarians who are willing to stand up for their communities' rights to have access to all types of material. They are vocal in the face of controversy, enduring verbal personal attacks and stressful confrontations. We hope that this book provides insight into how librarians protect the First Amendment in their communities. We hope this book encourages librarians to create thoughtful and strong collection development policies and reconsideration policies. Most important, we hope the stories in this book demonstrate the personal perspective that is necessary to support and strengthen library employees who must tirelessly defend even the most controversial material.

PART I

Sometimes We're Our Own Worst Enemy

When Library Employees Are Censors

For every reader, his or her book. For every book, its reader.
—S. R. RANGANATHAN

LIBRARIANS are the gatekeepers of information for the communities they serve. The First Amendment, the Freedom to Read Statement, and the American Library Association's Bill of Rights are documents that encourage librarians to swing the gates wide open and allow information to flow freely. It is a professional belief that American communities have diverse needs when it comes to library materials. Every reader in a community should be able to find himself or herself, without embarrassment or harassment, in a library book. If, however, librarians start closing gates and restricting information on the basis of their personal beliefs, appropriate service to these diverse populations does not exist. The chapters in this section may tell some of the most common stories found in today's libraries. The authors warn of the danger that exists when librarians censor library material before it even reaches the shelves.

CHAPTER 1

Where There Once Was None

LUCY BELLAMY

BEFORE BECOMING a librarian, I had heard stories about the lengths people go to in order to prevent others from reading certain books about certain topics or by certain authors. I had read Ray Bradbury's *Fahrenheit 451,* but in my mind the scenario depicted in Bradbury's famous book was a literary dramatization of what could happen in another place and time—certainly not within a few months of my being hired at a library.

My library serves the community of a private college that offers associate degrees, professional designation certificates, and a bachelor's degree in business management. Our library staff is a small, diverse group that includes a few professional librarians along with paraprofessionals. All of us understand the library's mission to support the college and its curriculum as well as our role of providing materials, resources, and services that enhance the research pursuits and educational goals of the students.

When I began working here I was just beginning my library program. Working while attending library school allowed me to gain practical experience in the concepts I was learning while completing my course work. It was a perfect fit. Although I was assigned to work primarily at the service desks (reference and circulation), I still got a sense of the materials our library offered. We have a great collection that supports research within the various program majors, as well as a wide range of general information resources. I could not have been a happier library school student.

I was soon promoted to another position where my primary responsibility was managing the collection. Previous staff members holding this position had little or no professional experience in this area. Their choices were not based on any library collection management principles. All that changed when I took on the position.

I loved being the "go-to" person in charge of what materials and resources our library offered our campus community. I took the responsibility seriously and set out to utilize the skills I learned in school that were necessary to ensure a collection of relevant materials for our users. I was already familiar with our constituency through my time spent at the service desks. I began studying the college catalog and reading the descriptions of the various courses. I reviewed the requirements of the program majors. I talked to faculty about their course objectives. I talked to students about our collection and asked them what we could do better to support their research and general information needs. I encouraged our users to make purchase recommendations for the collection. I walked the library stacks browsing the titles. I searched the online catalog. I reviewed the titles under the different subject headings. I wanted to have a full picture of the status of our collection. I also wanted to identify gaps in the collection.

Many of my coworkers understood what I did and supported the choices I made. Others who did the job before me, but remained on staff with other responsibilities, respected my approach to managing our collection and even said that having someone like me (someone with an academic background and professional interest) managing the collection made a positive difference in the quality of resources. As it turned out, not everyone shared this opinion. There was one staff member who, I later learned, did not like the choices I was making.

In addition to performing routine collection development tasks (review, selection, and acquisition of titles) I was also the first point of contact when books were received. This allowed me to conduct a more thorough review of each title before moving it into the technical processing queue. The next person to handle the books was our copy cataloger, who assigned the call number and cutter number. Once done, the books moved on to the next staff member for covering, tattle taping (security stripping), and spine labeling.

Around the time of Banned Books Week, I noticed that our collection did not include many books on censorship or intellectual property. I thought it would be appropriate to add a title or two that would provide a general discussion about these important concepts, particularly in a campus community where intellectual property is an issue of professional interest.

Within a short time several titles arrived that I quickly put into the queue. The benefit of working at a small library, and in an equally small work space, is that it is fairly easy to keep track of the progress of titles as they travel through the queue. I could look at the book cart of any staff member and determine how quickly those titles would be available for circulation. For a few titles, this journey through the queue would be delayed by an unforeseen force.

Our copy cataloger saw things differently than I did when it came to titles appropriate for our collection. I was advised during this time that she was becoming increasingly concerned (the word used was *offended*) about some of the newer books on intellectual property and censorship. She did not approach me to discuss her concerns. I learned of her concern later, through conversations with individual staff members who offered me this unsolicited information. These staff members repeatedly asked that our conversations remain anonymous.

Although surprised by this information, I was not initially concerned because I assumed that at some point she would approach me herself, but that was not the way she decided to handle it. This became apparent when I inadvertently discovered one of the books that I had purchased placed on our library director's desk with an attached note that read, in part, "Is this something that we really want our students to read?" The book was *Black Like You* by John Strausbaugh. The director was out of the office at the time, so I could not act on the note until I had the chance to speak with him. But in a short time another title, *Burning Books* by Haig Bosmajian, also seemed to "disappear" from the processing queue.

I approached several staff members (including the copy cataloger—feigning innocence when speaking with her so as not to let her know about the concerns other staff members had shared with me) in an attempt to locate the books. No one had an answer. I was later approached by a staff member who told me, under the condition of anonymity, that she might know something about the lost books. Without accusing the copy cataloger directly, she shared her suspicions about the copy cataloger's involvement with the disappearance of the books. The staff member told me that the copy cataloger had approached staff members with criticisms of my recent choices, labeling some of the selected titles "biased" and even "racist." I immediately recalled the provocative cover images—a minstrel in black face, and German soldiers in a "Sieg Heil" salute. I agreed that the images were unsettling, but they provided visual context to the discussion inside each title. Staff members told me that they had advised the copy cataloger to speak with me to resolve her concerns, but she refused.

In the meantime, I continued to do my job in spite of knowing how the copy cataloger felt about the recently received books. For a short time life went on without further incident, although the two books remained missing in action. I refused to approach her because it seemed unprofessional, reminiscent of behavior more appropriate for an elementary or junior high school playground (e.g., "Mary told me that Jane told her that you said . . . "). I spoke with the library director about the "rumors," and he agreed that it was up to the copy cataloger to approach me with her concerns. So I let it go, knowing that hard feelings were growing yet feeling helpless as to what to do to resolve the situation. Then another book acquisition pushed the stalled situation into high gear. I acquired an annotated edition of Harriet Beecher Stowe's *Uncle Tom's Cabin,* edited by scholars Henry Louis Gates Jr. and Hollis Robbins. This latest acquisition proved to be the final straw.

I was working at the reference desk one afternoon when a coworker approached to tell me that our copy cataloger was observed engaged in an agitated conversation with an instructor—something about books. She was speaking loud enough for others to hear parts of the conversation, which was described, in part, as something like this: "Here's another one of those books I was telling you about. She's just buying these books for her personal use. . . . If she wants to know about slavery, she should just come and ask me." I was in shock. The situation had reached the point where remaining silent was no longer an option.

I immediately went to the library director, accompanied by the staff member who had witnessed the conversation between the copy cataloger and the instructor. The staff member proceeded to reiterate what he had just seen and overheard. It was clear that this latest development was a sign that the situation was spiraling out of control. For me, there was no other way to interpret the situation than that I was being slandered within our college community. It no longer made sense to continue waiting for the copy cataloger to approach me with her concerns. I wanted to sit down immediately and have an open and honest discussion with her about her concerns, but the director saw things differently. Sensing that tensions (mine) were high, he advised me that it was not the time to confront her. He told me to go home for the rest of the day to calm down. It seemed like a reasonable suggestion, so I did as he recommended and went home. I was not prepared for the events that shortly followed.

I returned to work the next day to the news that the copy cataloger had been suspended. I asked the library director if he had met with her to discuss the current situation. He said he had not. I asked if there was another reason for this action. He said he would not discuss the details. I was confused but deferred to his discretion.

Later that day I was once again called into the director's office. He told me that the copy cataloger would not be returning to the library; he had made the decision to terminate her employment. I asked if his decision was based on the situation involving the books. He said it was not. I asked if he discussed the conversation with the instructor or her note and about the book she left on his desk. He said he had not. Again I was confused. He expressed surprise at my reaction and wondered why I wasn't more relieved that the situation was now, according to him, resolved. But how could I be relieved if her concerns were not addressed and the books were still missing? He told me that it was no longer my concern.

I left his office thinking that the outcome should have been different. It seems strange in retrospect, but I decided to review the collection development policy to see if I had missed something. Did we miss the part that discussed how to handle a request for reconsideration of library materials? I was both surprised and disappointed to find that the policy did not address this type of situation at all. Unfortunately, at this point there was really nothing more that could be done to change the outcome of this particular situation, but it was within my power to do something that would prevent a repeat of this situation in the future. I immediately went to work revising the policy to include steps to guide staff and library users through the reconsideration of library materials process. When I asked staff members if any library materials in the library had ever been challenged before, they told me no, that this was the first time. Well, that sort of explained why the discussion was not included in the current policy. No one had *ever* challenged materials before the problems we had faced with these books. They, like me, never imagined that a reconsideration of library materials could happen in an environment where art, design, and creativity were associated with freedom—as a state of mind, being, and thought.

Looking back on this experience I can see that it was a "once in a lifetime" event. I was familiar with the concept of censorship, but this experience gave me a lifelong teachable moment. Although I felt differently at the time, in retrospect I'm glad that it happened. Still, I never would have imagined that it would happen to me so early in my career: I was just beginning my second semester of library school and had recently joined (within the year) the library staff. They say that "baptism by fire" is one way to learn something fast. This definitely was a learning experience, for *everyone*. The positive spin is that it resulted in a much stronger collection development policy. Had this revised collection development policy and the procedure been in place before this incident, perhaps the copy cataloger would still have her job. I guess there is something to be said about things happening for a reason, but I will save that discussion for another time.

CHAPTER 2

Well-Intentioned Censorship Is Still Censorship

The Challenge of Public Library Employees

RON CRITCHFIELD AND DAVID M. POWELL

THE DIFFERENCES between personal values and professional ethics often cause a struggle within oneself. In the case of our library, the Jessamine County Public Library (JCPL) in Nicholasville, Kentucky, this type of struggle began within our walls and eventually extended into the community we serve. The facts presented below were made public during the latter part of 2009 by news coverage and literature distributed in our community concerning two former JCPL employees who decided a library book was inappropriate for minors.

Our story begins with a book perceived to be obscene by a library employee working as a circulation associate at JCPL. The employee brought the item to the attention of David Powell, circulation manager, who listened to her concerns and instructed her to submit an official request for reconsideration of the book. Subsequently, the employee submitted the request to the collection development committee.

The book in question was *The League of Extraordinary Gentlemen: Black Dossier,* written by Alan Moore and illustrated by Kevin O'Neill. The staff member found the book to be pornographic in nature and as such inappropriate for circulation by the library. After reading the book and literature about the book, the committee members ruled to retain the challenged item in the collection because it met all criteria outlined in JCPL's collection development policy. The committee also cited a variety of supportive factors:

- Moore, a highly respected author of graphic novels (e.g., *Watchmen, V for Vendetta, Swamp Thing*)
- listed #2 in the 2007 Top Ten Graphic Novels, by *Time* magazine
- listed #2 in DC Comics' "30 Essential Graphic Novels"
- won the 2007 Eagle Award for "Favourite Original Graphic Novel"
- well reviewed by *Booklist* and *Publisher's Weekly* (starred review)
- in more than a thousand library collections, including at least twelve other Kentucky libraries
- could be purchased in nearby Lexington bookstores such as Joseph-Beth Booksellers, Comic Interlude, Barnes and Noble Booksellers, and Borders

Unsatisfied with the results from the review committee, the employee decided to check out the book and keep it in her work locker so that no other person could have the item. In an attempt to keep the book from others, this employee set in motion a cycle of checkouts and renewals that followed standard circulation procedures. She checked out the item, renewed it twice, checked in the item, then again checked it out and continued this process. When the library director, Ron Critchfield, learned of this practice, it seemed odd to him that the person who previously wanted the item removed from the collection now had checked it out more than any other customer. Uncertain exactly what was going on, Critchfield discussed the issue with Powell, and they decided Powell would check on the item's status every now and then.

Months passed and someone placed a hold on the book. Powell monitored the status of the item as its due date approached to make sure it was returned. It is the library's policy that once an item with a hold on it is returned, the library computer system immediately reserves the book for the customer who requested the hold. Unfortunately, the item was not returned. As a result, the person who placed the hold request on the item never got the chance to access the book. Powell brought this news to Critchfield's attention and explained that another employee, also then a circulation associate, removed the hold from the item being monitored, and then the employee who initially challenged the item checked out the book again. Something was odd . . . nay, wrong. The employment of the two employees was terminated for exercising censorship and restricting the freedom of others on the basis of their personal beliefs.

The former employees then crafted, or found themselves placed in, a narrative focused on the valiant stand made by two Christian women to protect the children of the community from pornographic materials distributed at JCPL—because parents have busy lives and need help parenting their children. Given this biblical story around which to rally, the media fire ignited, setting ablaze the first anti-library narrative.

In October 2009, WTVQ-36 in Lexington, Kentucky, ran a television news report titled "Librarians Won't Give Child 'Porn' Book."[1] The media was invited to JCPL by those crafting the anti-JCPL narrative. In this report both former circulation associates provided statements and began publicizing their cause. The reporter noted, "The two women say they were fired last month when they wouldn't let a young girl check out a book from The League of Extraordinary Gentleman series. Now, both women say they're less concerned with their jobs and more concerned with keeping material like this out of children's hands." One of the former employees had this to say about the removal of the hold from the item: "My friend . . . had brought it to me on Wednesday, and she said 'look at this book, it's filthy and it's on hold for an eleven-year-old girl,' and I said well okay, let's take it off hold." The reporter concluded by stating, "The women say parents these days are swamped and it's far too easy for a child to check out a book without them ever knowing. The women hope the library will reconsider their policies to make sure children aren't checking out inappropriate materials."

In addition to the television reporting of the anti-JCPL narrative, a flyer from the group was distributed around the county. The vast majority of information contained in the flyer was misinformation.

The widely circulated narrative in opposition to the library began: "On Sep 23, 2009, two library employees were let go from the Jessamine County Public Library (JCPL) for refusing to allow an eleven year old girl access to the book *League of Extraordinary Gentlemen: Black Dossier,* a graphic novel which contains lewd pictures of men and women in sexual situations." One can see the use of emotive argument here to portray the former library employees as champions and not censors—to portray them as justified, righteous, and concerned citizens "let go" by JCPL for "doing right."

Another aspect of the narrative was that graphic novels are synonymous with things pornographic: "Books located in the graphic novel section of the library contain pornographic material including pictures of nude men and women in sexual situations. These items can be checked out by juveniles on their own accounts, without parental consent or knowledge." This juxtaposition of graphic novels with pornographic material sent a false understanding to the minds of those unfamiliar with graphic novels and led to these items being associated with pornography. Also, the latter sentence was a misleading statement presented as fact. At

JCPL parents must sign for juveniles seventeen and under to have a card, and parents have complete monitoring privileges.

The flyer ended the narrative in the same way the initial news report concluded: "We urge residents of Jessamine County to get involved in letting the library know that such material being available to minors is not acceptable in this community. We need to protect children from adult obscene material." It is important to note that there is no statutory authority in Kentucky for public libraries to act in place of parents. In fact, public libraries open themselves to lawsuits if they try to act in loco parentis. It is JCPL's position, and should be the position of any public library, that parents know best what is acceptable for their children, and that any limits should be set by the parents—not by the library staff.

In November 2009, more than one hundred citizens attended the library's monthly board meeting to provide comments regarding the situation. Each speaker was given two minutes to share her or his opinions with the members of the library board and library management. The opinions expressed were evenly divided in support of and opposed to JCPL's position against censorship. Anti-library comments ranged from an evangelist yelling about the library shelving pornography to a teenager wanting the library to protect her and others from harmful materials. Library supporters included a woman recounting how limitations at her childhood library stifled her growth as a reader and another person sharing her minister father's strong belief in the First Amendment and urging others to stand up for it.

One speaker presented a petition calling for the removal of not only *The League of Extraordinary Gentlemen: Black Dossier* but also Chuck Palahniuk and Ron White's comedy CD *You Can't Fix Stupid*. In the months that followed, some people who signed the petition contacted the library and said they regretted signing it before becoming fully informed about the issue.

The most disappointing and troubling occurrences were the personal attacks on the library director and other library employees. These assaults came via persons physically coming to the library, written letters to the library and local papers, e-mails, and phone calls. JCPL librarians were accused of becoming desensitized to harmful material and even of being pedophiles looking to identify children who might be susceptible to sexual advances. One angry community member went as far as to confront the library director and threaten physical violence.

Faced with a vocal minority speaking out against the library, and an onslaught of reporters seeking a story, JCPL management communicated the following guidelines to JCPL employees for dealing with these internal situations:

Speak with one voice, with one spokesperson: When you receive inquiries outside the realm of your job duties, such as questions about library customers, library staff, former library staff, or the management and direction of the library, you are not to respond. All such outside inquiries should be readdressed to the director. Offer the inquirer the director's business card and let anyone know that they can feel free to come and knock on the director's door, or e-mail, or send a letter, or call the director. Speaking only to the director removes the awkwardness for employees and eliminates potentially detrimental situations in which employees might say something inappropriate or counter to the mission of the library.

Emphasize library confidentiality: As an employee of the library you must not improperly disclose confidential information about library customers, employees, or library business at any time.

Given the inaccurate information spread about the library within the community, we managed the external misinformation situation with the following guidelines:

Allow only one spokesperson: As previously mentioned, this removed the multiplicity of voices saying who knows what.

Publicity: A public awareness blitz emphasized community assets of the public library. We spent money on posters and advertisements to show the importance of the public library.

Spread the truth: The local newspaper published an opinion article by the director concerning intellectual freedom. JCPL created a brochure with the facts about parental knowledge, consent, and monitoring privileges—highly effective in educating those misled by the opposing narrative.

Do not be drawn in—remain above the fray: Do not argue, do not offer point-counterpoint debate, do not enter the online discussions. Be courteous to all callers (in person, on the phone, via e-mail), offer copies of your policies, and thank them for their feedback.

If we can stress only one point, it is the last one: do not be drawn in—remain above the fray. Although it is difficult not to defend yourself and your library by publicly arguing against your accusers, such action only fuels the fires, excites the media, and brings you down to the same level as those circulating misinformation. Take a deep breath and smile. Then show the community how great your library is and leave the arguing to others.

Another thing to remember is that public libraries serve *all* members of a community, and it is important to listen to every citizen's concerns. The Jessamine County residents who expressed displeasure over the materials in the collection or the dismissal of the library employees were a minority of the county's total population, but we listened to their concerns and suggestions. Many of the concerns involved the shelf placement of the graphic novels. After researching how other libraries shelve graphic novels and after careful deliberation, the library management decided to relocate the graphic novels to the adult and young adult nonfiction sections.

As in most situations involving censorship of library materials, the persons bringing the challenge are acting on what they feel is right and socially responsible. The library employees who were terminated did not intentionally challenge First Amendment rights in their quest to protect children from harmful materials. It is logical to conclude that their actions took place because they believed their ideas were right. It is unclear, though, if they really understood what role libraries serve in a community and what First Amendment liberties they denied to others through their actions.

Public libraries exist to provide access to ideas, information, and cultural opportunities essential to a literate and educated society. Foundational to this mission are the concepts of free access and user privacy. Library users must feel safe to seek out and explore library resources without barriers. Those working in the library must facilitate such information seeking by assisting users without judgment and by assuring privacy in their transactions. Library employees must be able to separate their personal convictions from their professional duty to safeguard and respect the freedoms of *every* library user. Although a library employee may be a well-intentioned citizen who wishes to protect users from material he or she deems harmful, such an employee becomes a censor when restricting access to library material. No matter the justification, well-intentioned censorship is still censorship.

NOTE

1. Cate Slattery, "Librarians Won't Give Child 'Porn' Book," ABC 36, www.wtvq.com/news/672-librarians-wont-give-child-porn-book.

CHAPTER 3

If I Don't Buy It, They Won't Come

PEGGY KANEY

IT STARTED with a boy—three boys, actually. I first "met" them in 2001 via a book review of *Rainbow Boys* by Alex Sanchez. The three boys, Nelson, Kyle, and Jason, are characters in the book and are true-to-life teens living lives that include the typical concerns of friends, family, love, and school. In her review, Betty Evans described the themes of the book: "ecstasy, heartache, and humor of first love . . . having what it takes to stand up and be proud of who you are."[1] Unlike other teen romances that revolve around boy-meets-girl, Nelson, Kyle, and Jason happen to be gay and are falling in love with each other. Other than that, the heartache, the angst, and the joys are typical teen fare and very familiar to anyone charged with building a library collection for this demographic.

At the time I read the review, I was the coordinator for youth services for a small public library in a rural environment in a conservative state. Even though my county tended to vote toward the center, I knew there was a strong possibility that someone would be offended that this book was available to our teen readers. I recalled an earlier event when a woman from the community bought a book from the library book sale table and promptly threw it in the trash can nearest the circulation desk, letting us know that her actions were a response to the gay characters in the book. She further explained that she had formerly lived in New York City and had seen firsthand the effect that such materials could have on the decisions and actions of young people. At the time, I was amazed that she felt so strongly and not only told the library staff about her views but also acted on them in such a public manner.

When I came across the review for *Rainbow Boys,* I tried to balance that trash can memory with the positive review that was in front of me.

Had the characters not been gay, I most likely would have ordered the book without a second thought. But the very real concern that the same patron (or another with a similar point of view) would discover the book on the shelves and challenge it gave me pause. The final lines of Evans's review haunted me: "There will no doubt be challenges to *Rainbow Boys,* much like the challenges to Judy Blume's *Forever.* . . . But please, have the courage to make it available to those who need it—it can open eyes and change lives.[2]

I set the review aside. I lacked the courage to select the book for the collection and to face the challenge that might follow. I discussed my decision with our library branch manager, who sincerely thanked me for not selecting the title. She agreed that we did not need to invite a challenge. Simply put, if we did not buy this book, the critics would not come. We could avoid an uncomfortable scene by just ignoring this title—by just convincing ourselves that no one would miss it.

The decision was made, my supervisor approved my actions, but I felt guilty. I have always felt confident of myself as an accepting, open-minded person, but I caved to outside pressure when a tough choice had to be made. I knew that I had let fear guide my nonselection instead of following our library's collection development criteria, professional reviews, and knowledge of the community we served. I was willing to turn my back on the information needs of a silent population rather than risk the wrath of a potential critic. I knew I had let our patrons down.

I conveniently tucked the book review away in the recesses of my brain until the topic was brought back to the forefront courtesy of an anonymous message that appeared in the library some time later. A folded piece of paper was found among other returned items in the book drop by one of the other library staff members. She opened it to find a handwritten note scrawled on a photocopy of a page of young adult book reviews from the *Lambda Book Report.* The note requested that the library recognize the fact that lesbian, gay, bisexual, transgender, questioning, and queer (LGBTQ) youth frequented the library, and the note let us know that their needs were being ignored.[3] Because I was the selector for youth materials, the note made its way to my desk. Several of the reviewed titles were highlighted, and the note begged that these titles be considered for the library collection. "I'm not the only one who wants these," the anonymous writer told us. "There are more of us than you may think, and we need these books!" A quick investigation told me that the *Lambda Book Report* was a publication of the Lambda Literary Foundation, which featured reviews of LGBTQ titles of various genres. Despite my efforts to ignore them, characters like Nelson, Kyle, and Jason would not be forgotten. Quietly, they had returned to my consciousness with a plea to let their story be *available to those who need it.*

The *Rainbow Boys* won, and I bought the book—but not before I was fairly certain that I would be leaving that position for a new job as an academic librarian. My short-term status gave me heightened courage, for I knew it was unlikely that I would be the one to face the critics if they came. Though not altogether proud of my motives, I was pleased that even in my spinelessness I could start the ball rolling. Although I wasn't forthcoming about my choice with my supervisor, I admitted to a coworker that I had ordered the title, and we discussed the appropriateness of the choice, especially in response to the anonymous note. From her support of the selection decision, I knew that someone else would be picking up where I left off. Shortly after I switched jobs, I returned to the library and found the book on the shelf. Reassured that I had made the right choice, I wondered about the book's future readers and hoped that I had helped to satisfy the need identified by the anonymous note.

A few years passed. By this time, I was working at a university library as well as occasionally teaching classes. As the instructor in a youth literature course for education majors, I found myself recommending *Rainbow Boys* and its two sequels to a gay university student. The student had recently "come out" to his advisor in the College of Education and was struggling to come to terms with what this meant in his future professional teaching career. He wanted to be able to recommend books to his future students if they were questioning their own gender roles. We talked at length about youth literature and how lost he had felt during junior high and high school when coming to terms with his own sexuality. After reading *Rainbow Boys,* he regretted not knowing about books like it when he was a teen. I shared my guilt at being afraid to select LGBTQ titles and through our discussions felt both a proxy forgiveness and a conviction never to let fear guide my professional decisions again.

I would like to think that times have changed, and that other librarians are currently doing a better job of providing LGBTQ materials. A recent blog post helped me to realize the impact that my actions may have had, as well as the actions of librarians that self-censor all over the country. A gay fifteen-year-old, Brent, posted to the *Pinched Nerve* blog on June 15, 2010, about his experience looking for LGBTQ titles in his school library:

> When I set out to find more LGBT titles, I turned to my school's library. Honestly? It was pathetic. There was not one single LGBT novel. . . . When I asked her [the librarian] about it, she replied,

"This is a school library. If you are looking to read inappropriate titles, go to a book store." Uhm, how in the hell is LGBT YA lit "inappropriate"? I mean, think about it. Let it register: The librarian claimed LGBT novels were inappropriate, yet she approved of books that had heterosexual sex. Yeah, she was being gay-cist![4]

Brent shares his experience in next trying his public library, to no avail. He then dives into the heart of the matter, which is the fact that many librarians are self-censoring. Regardless of their reasons, their decisions lead to a hole in the collection and underserved patrons.

The world needs more librarians who serve the purpose of finding the right book to put in the right person's lap. Not librarians who think that they can decide what's "inappropriate" and what's not, based on their personal prejudices. There are tons of gay teens, struggling to find a group to fit in. LGBT YA lit helps us find out that no, we aren't alone and no, we aren't worthless or disgusting. It helps us discover that we are part of a group. The LGBT group.

One of the responses to Brent's posting was from Scott, a school library media specialist: "I have colleagues who will not order GLBT literature because they are worried about challenges from parents and organizations. Don't let the folks in my profession fool you or anybody! Self-censorship happens all the time in libraries when materials are being ordered and it needs to stop!"

These words stung, because I knew that I had been one of the librarians who had dropped the ball. It was irrelevant that my heart was in the right place, that I had not had any personal problems with including the material—my decision not to purchase the book was self-censorship. My self-censorship based on my fear resulted in a lack of materials for people who wanted and needed them and was detrimental to the goal of building a library collection that truly served the whole community.

As it turned out, sometime after *Rainbow Boys* was added to the public library collection and after I had moved to the academic library position, the critics did come. I learned from my former coworker that a complaint was initiated by a parent of a young adult patron who didn't feel that the book was appropriate and should not be available for circulation. A formal challenge was issued, the local reconsideration process ran its course, but the title was eventually retained in the collection. *Rainbow Boys* survived the local book challenge, but it quietly and mysteriously disappeared from the shelves nonetheless. As of this writing, the book and its sequels may be easily borrowed from another branch in the library district, but they cannot be found by browsing the local library shelves. The book may have disappeared at the hands of a disgruntled critic who failed to remove it via the official channel or a library employee who didn't want to take the chance on further challenges, or perhaps it was spirited away by a young patron who was too embarrassed to check out the book. It is unlikely that the events that led to its disappearance will ever be known.

As is the case in many locations, there is still work to be done at that public library to create a collection that meets the needs of all the patrons, including those from the LGBTQ community. For my part, I will be donating a copy of *Rainbow Boys* to the local library very soon—in penance for my past actions, and in the hopes that it will be *available to those who need it.*

NOTES

1. Betty S. Evans, Review of *Rainbow Boys,* by Alex Sanchez, *School Library Journal* 47 (October 2001): 169.

2. Ibid.

3. Note on terminology: In my readings, I have seen the following acronyms used: LGBT, GLBT, LGBTQ, and GLBTQ for the gay, lesbian, bisexual, transgender, questioning, and queer community. I have addressed the question of acronym preference to various individuals who identify with these categories and have not found a standard preference. Therefore, I chose not to standardize the acronym within this work; instead, for references to individuals or organizations, I use the acronym that was selected by that individual or organization. In cases where I inserted an acronym, I used LGBTQ.

4. *Pinched Nerves* blog: http://janettrumble.wordpress.com.

CHAPTER 4

Mixed-Up Ethics

SUSAN PATRON

WE EXAMINE case studies of challenged books, of librarians holding firm to principles of intellectual freedom. We champion authors who speak up for the rights of children. We rely on organizations like the American Library Association to collect statistics, support beleaguered staff during a challenge, and help libraries highlight and celebrate the First Amendment. As a profession, we are fiercely and visibly protective of the freedom to read.

But what about librarians who do not acquire certain books because they suspect they'll be controversial? Guided by fear and the anticipation of "problems," they select materials with the avoidance of confrontation in mind. Because it is difficult to monitor or measure this form of self-censorship, it is particularly insidious. And I believe it is not uncommon.

These librarians may admit to personal discomfort in using the book, or point out a sense of obligation to shield young readers from certain topics or words. When *The Higher Power of Lucky* became controversial because of the use of the word *scrotum* (in context of a dog being bitten by a rattlesnake), I tried to figure out what harm could come to readers. Would they go wild with this word, shouting it as a playground obscenity? Perhaps they would turn it into an insult: "Get off my skateboard, you miserable scrotum!" Or maybe they would upset a more sedate generation: "Hey, grandma, check out that dog's scrotum!" None of it seemed likely to me, and more funny than awful were it to occur.

Those cautious librarians have their ethics mixed up. They have appointed themselves, inappropriately, in loco parentis, as the legal representative of the parent. It is not the public librarian's job to protect children from language or moral dilemmas raised in literature. On the contrary, I believe most of us are driven by our conviction that books, particularly fiction, are the safest, most deeply affecting way for children to encounter and explore moral ambiguity. Our obligation as librarians is to defend and protect children's freedom to read, and to make sure they have access to rich and extensive collections in public libraries.

Number VII of ALA's Code of Ethics states, "We distinguish between our personal convictions and professional duties and do not allow our personal beliefs to interfere with fair representation of the aims of our institutions or the provision of access to their . . . resources."[1] Ethical librarians do not presume to withhold controversial children's or young adult literature from an entire community of young readers whose sensibilities and maturity vary widely. Ethical librarians provide the material along with expert readers' advisory based on their own extensive reading. They redirect and guide colleagues who make selection decisions from a position of fear or of inappropriate protectiveness. I am ever grateful to those librarians and to the profession.

NOTE

1. American Library Association, "Code of Ethics of the American Library Association," www.ala.org/ala/issuesadvocacy/proethics/codeofethics/codeethics.cfm

PART II

How Dare You Recommend This Book to a Child

Reading Levels and Sophisticated Topics

All these people talk so eloquently about getting back to good old-fashioned values. Well, as an old poop I can remember back to when we had those old-fashioned values, and I say let's get back to the good old-fashioned First Amendment of the good old-fashioned Constitution of the United States—and to hell with the censors! Give me knowledge or give me death!

—KURT VONNEGUT

PROTECTING children from harm is a common ideal found across cultures around the world. When it comes to ideas and information, the professional ethics that guide librarians require the librarian to be free of judgment when it comes to allowing or discouraging a child's access to library material. The authors in this section have all encountered complaints about library material by parents. Each author's experience includes creative solutions for educating parents and children, eventually resulting in retaining library material for continued use in the library.

CHAPTER 5

Clue-less in Portland

NATASHA FORRESTER

MY MOST frustrating and simultaneously funny censorship challenge experience involved the book *Minerva Clark Gets a Clue* by Karen Karbo.

I'm a youth librarian in a neighborhood branch of the Multnomah County Library System in Portland, Oregon. I co-coordinate an after-school book group for fourth through eighth grades with a local private school. The school librarian and I select books that will work for the whole group (which realistically is made up of fourth- through sixth-graders) or for two age groups, fourth and fifth grades and sixth through eighth grades. After reading *Minerva Clark Gets a Clue,* we selected it because it was a high-interest book and had good reviews from *School Library Journal, Horn Book,* and *Booklist.* Additionally, the author is local and agreed to do a visit with the group, either by phone or in person. The book is even set in Portland.

A week or so after the book was given out, the school librarian called to let me know she'd received a complaint from the parent of one of the fifth-grade students. The mother had objected to several things in the book. In one scene, the main character's older "wild girl" cousin and her friends are portrayed as smoking, and the main character tells them cigarettes will kill them. The mother thought that showing characters smoking would make more of an impact on the readers than the main character's message. She also thought that the book mocks the magazine *American Girl.* Finally, the book has the main character saying "the f-word" (the character does not actually say "f*ck," she says "the f-word"). The mother wanted us to stop using the book with the book group and to be sure it was not available through the school library.

It was explained to the parent that she could choose to not have her child read the book for the month, and the child would not attend the meeting at which the book was discussed. The book was retained in the school library (the mother didn't actually challenge it in the public library), and a permission slip was created for all parents to sign in which they either gave permission for their child to read books beyond their grade level (per the book's MARC record) or restricted them to read-only books that had their grade level or below listed in the book's MARC record. Most parents gave permission, with only two parents choosing to restrict their child's reading to grade level provided in the book's MARC record.

The author came to the school and gave a school-wide assembly. According to the school librarian, the parent did not object to having her child attend the assembly. The student did in fact attend, with no problems or comments from the parent about the appropriateness of the book to the author during the visit. There were no further issues with that parent, because she pulled her child from the book group.

We don't actually use the permission slip any more; we just used it that one year, but we do make sure the book's MARC record labels indicate the book's grade level.

CHAPTER 6

Vixens, Banditos, and Finding Common Ground

ALISA C. GONZALEZ

LIVING IN a border city, one finds that the lines between countries and cultures become indistinguishable at times. El Paso, Texas, and Cuidad Juárez, Mexico, are separated by the width of a freeway, the Rio Grande, and a fence. The border between the countries at times feels very thin, and at other times the significant differences between countries and cultures become obvious. Spanish is the predominant language in some areas of El Paso, and every sign in a public establishment is in both English and Spanish. Thousands of people cross the border from both sides every day to work. Each area of El Paso is an ever-moving point on a spectrum in the melding of border culture. There is a Mexican current running throughout the area.

It takes a closer drive along the border to see the stark differences between the two countries. Yellow and pink houses without electricity dot the hills and streets of Juárez. People wait by the Rio Grande to cross the border when Border Patrol officials are not looking, with hopes to better their lives, escaping violent conditions and high unemployment. At times it seems like the citizens of El Paso are all part of a large metropolitan area with the reflection of each side of the border visible—opposite but similar. With this larger culture in mind, our libraries in El Paso are responsive by including a greater than normal proportion of Spanish-language materials and programming. This diversity leads to unique collection situations in a multicultural city.

I worked in a large district branch in the West Side of El Paso. As with any city, each section of the city has different personalities. The West Side is full of transplants from other states and countries. The neighborhoods are filled with U.S. Army officers, Drug Enforcement Administration personnel, customs agents, and businesspeople who work in the Juárez *maquiladoras* (export assembly plants). It is common to see people of many ethnicities and to hear many different languages spoken. In the public library where I worked, I often heard Spanish mixed with English from both patrons and library workers. This mix of people led to a sense that the community was very aware of the similarities and differences in all cultures.

I was also a transplant to the area. My husband's job had transferred him to the Juárez operations of a U.S. corporation. Experiencing two cultures at once can be very challenging to a newcomer. My husband felt a little culture shock, but it was nothing that time didn't resolve. Having grown up in a bicultural home with an Irish American mother and Mexican father allowed me to transition to the El Paso area faster than other transplants. Although El Paso felt different from Ohio, I was confident that an Irish-looking girl with black hair and green eyes could transact easily with both Spanish and English speakers. Although I was a newcomer, El Paso seemed like home to me.

DEVELOPING COLLECTIONS AND CENSORSHIP

In our library, the collection reflected the use of the local Hispanic population. Books for all ages, DVDs, periodicals, and other materials for Spanish speakers were representative of our outreach to the community. Also, to serve the population we stocked fotonovelas—small magazines that can be moral and sensational in scope. They are moralistic in the lesson of the story, warning people of the bad consequences of sinful behavior. They narrate the struggles of the working class and the pitfalls that lead to unhappiness. They also feature an exciting story to keep the reader's attention and a sensationalistic picture on the front cover to draw one into reading them. Scantily clad women, hardworking people, and men with guns are the usual stars of the show. Some fotonovelas are racier than others, featuring sex and violence. No matter what the focus, fotonovelas are a must-have item for a Spanish collection supporting low-level literacy.

Before the branch opened, the librarians and staff had many discussions about the best placement of the fotonovelas. Certain of their characteristics could bring objections at our branch—a concern that was not necessarily relevant at other branches with greater Hispanic populations. The small fotonovelas wound up on the bottom shelf in the back of the Spanish collection. We agreed that it would be easier for the older women to reach them in this location. Also, we knew keeping the fotonovelas organized would be impossible, so we decided that they would be shelved best in a box on the bottom shelf. Could it be that we were unconsciously censoring and hiding this element of our collection? At the least, perhaps, we were undervaluing the positive aspects of the fotonovelas.

Some days, a librarian at the reference desk can see a story unfold. This day was no exception. I was watching the people in the library and became aware of a mother with children. She was conservatively dressed, covered in clothing from head to toe. Ahead of their mother, two preteen boys ran in two directions away from her. She was loudly giving them orders as they were running away, not really listening to her.

I went about my business on that otherwise quiet day, answering questions at the reference desk and working on desk projects. Sensing someone approaching, I looked up to see the modestly dressed woman approaching me with a fotonovela in her hand. She loudly announced, "Do you think this is something that a fourteen-year-old should be looking at?" I looked at the fotonovela. The cover featured a stereotypical sultry Latina with a tight corset and ripped-up skirt and a sinister-looking man viewing her lecherously. The mother claimed that the novela was completely inappropriate for a library with children. This had been the first time that she let her kids roam the library, she explained, and this was the result of her lapse in judgment. She also felt that a "comic" had no literary value and no place in a library. She questioned why materials such as fotonovelas should be purchased at all for the collection with public funds. Her children were behind her, and the older boy had a bit of a red face. The mother wanted all of the fotonovelas removed from our collection.

Her voice kept rising with emotion. She was visibly shaken and I asked her to come back to my office. Clearly such an interaction would be better handled away from the public. The other patrons who were nearby were paying attention at this point, and she agreed to come to my office alone.

My immediate response was to try to defuse the situation before referring the woman to the branch manager or director. My response started out with the boilerplate answers we provide users who protest the inclusion of certain types material or specific titles in the collection. As librarians we are all aware that the standard answers sometimes create angry patrons. Training and experience require us to temper a defensive attitude, which is not always easy to do. "We try to have something for every reader," I repeated. "Sometimes we all are made uncomfortable with what is in our collection," I reassured her. She wasn't buying it, so I tried another angle.

I decided to address the material in a cultural context, hoping that she would make the connection to her own culture. "It's a cultural thing. Every culture has its own way of expressing itself and we need to be respectful of that fact. We don't have to agree, but we should try to understand.

These fotonovelas are really important for some patrons. Your son just stumbled upon them."

"Well, maybe that's the problem with that culture," she hissed. "Pregnant teens, promiscuity . . . it's all sinful. Look at how many of them have babies," she stated matter-of-factly. She went on and on about pregnant Hispanic teens straining the welfare system. It was an argument that made me internally roll my eyes.

Not looking traditionally Mexican can be a blessing and a curse. I feel like an undercover agent, since not many people can pinpoint my ethnicity. I told her that I had been raised by a traditional Mexican father and that I did not see these as our cultural values. I reminded her that there are pregnant teens and disagreements about some sexual behaviors in all populations. She claimed that she too "had Mexican blood." This term, "Mexican blood," can sometimes be a distancing term. It is an acknowledgment that a person has a distant Mexican relative, but this patron was clearly indicating that she did not think she was raised like a Mexican American. She seemed to be very irritated about the fact that she had Mexican blood. She made it clear that she brought her children to the library at part of homeschooling them, which she did to keep them from what she deemed immoral.

From that point, I started to see that this was a complicated issue. Apparently she wasn't fond of the Mexican culture. She was also terrified that her fourteen-year-old son was growing up. He was doing what any fourteen-year-old boy would do if the opportunity presented itself. In a previous job, I had worked as a community educator for Planned Parenthood. I understood puberty and the strong feelings that it elicited from parents. Sometimes I felt puberty was just as difficult for the parent as the child. Remembering this, I instantly understood her better and felt a lot of sympathy.

All of a sudden, I felt free to abandon the script that we use when speaking about challenged materials. I needed to find common ground with her. I told her that I was a mother also, and I understood wanting your child to have the same values as the rest of the family. I understood wanting to protect your children and not expose them too early to outside influences. Then she said, "It's just so hard. . . . I don't know what else to do." She got teary. I could see that the fotonovela wasn't the only thing that had her upset. It was just the breaking point. I immediately felt a great deal of sympathy for her. We were women and mothers. We both got up every day and tried to do our best. We both had strong opinions and beliefs. Despite our many differences, we were also similar.

I didn't really know what else to do because the interaction suddenly changed. She began to vent about her life. She was a good mother who cared more than anything about her family. She felt she was losing control of her children as they were growing up. She was torn between holding on to them and letting them learn lessons on their own. She truly was afraid. She continued to talk about things that concerned her with today's world.

At a break in the conversation, I decided to bring the discussion slowly back to the matter at hand. I gave her the library's form for requesting a review of materials in our collection. I asked her to fill it out because her opinion was important to us. She filled it out, asking me questions about being a librarian and our library in general. I was incredibly joyous to talk about something other than the bodice-busting novela.

After she completed the form, we both stood up to leave the office. I extended my hand to shake hers. She walked over to me and gave me a long, tight hug. She thanked me for listening to her. From that day on, I would see her in the library here and there. We would chat when we saw each other, but she never asked me about the fotonovelas, and I never brought them up again.

ACKNOWLEDGING CULTURE

From first appearance, we couldn't have been two more different people. Everything about us was a contrast, physically and mentally. When she first approached the desk, I believed that we couldn't possibly agree on anything. We were from two different worlds and cultures, but we found common ground in our common human experience and not physical manifestations of our beliefs and mores. It is important for librarians to understand and acknowledge that we may be culturally different from the people who enter our doors.

For public services librarians, the best part of working in a library is the daily interactions with our users, regardless of age, gender, or ethnicity. I certainly have had other experiences with challenged material that have not been smooth. People who feel the need to censor often build high walls and will not change their opinions. This patron just needed to be heard; she needed someone to really listen. I learned that objections to materials are many times related to fears, justified or not, built around something the patron strongly believes. It is not about the library material itself but about the tensions that arise when cultures (religious, ethnic, or other) meet. That moment, when we found common ground and an emotional confrontation was defused, continues to be one of my most meaningful and successful interactions with a patron.

CHAPTER 7

Long Live the King (Novels)!

ANGELA PAUL

TEN YEARS ago, during my first week at a middle school—within my first two weeks of being in Wichita, Kansas, actually—a woman walked into my library, passed by me, and headed straight to a bookshelf of paperback fiction. I followed her and asked if I could help her find something. She was looking for Stephen King, she said, because she helped the librarian last year remove all of the King novels, but there were a couple that were missing at the time of the removal and she wanted to make sure they had been found and removed.

The previous librarian was a certified teacher, not a professional librarian, and I believe my training in library science helped with my reply. We commiserated together about the trend of publishers to print trashy fiction designed to incite, thrill, and excite instead of upholding moral values, along with the prevalence of numbered series and set books at all age levels. How valuable are novels that all seem to have the same plot and theme?

Then I explained that boys tend to stop reading in middle school and read less throughout high school and college. This trend is similar for girls, but more girls than boys tend to be readers. If children read in middle school, they are more likely to read throughout their life. Even if all the books they read are basically alike, if they keep reading they learn to appreciate stories more thought provoking and interesting.

I told this woman that, if a boy wanted to read nothing but Stephen King, I would not stop him. Stephen King's stories are full of strong female characters and characters who face challenges and fears. Most fiction, even horror, has some redeeming value as a story, and if reading such "trash" keeps people reading, then they should be encouraged to read it.

She actually thanked me for my information. I don't even know if she had a student at the school that year, but I did not see her again. This is the closest encounter I had with a parent wanting to censor a book or an author.

CHAPTER 8

Parent Concern about Classroom Usage Spills Over into School Library

LAURIE TREAT

AT OUR high school, new English reading classroom book sets or adoption materials were selected during the 2008/09 school year. One English teacher chose to teach *Slaughterhouse Five,* and a set of classroom books was ordered. In the fall of 2009 a parent voiced his concern to one of the high school assistant principals, stating the repeated reference to bestiality found in the book.

The assistant principal assured the parent that his child would not be required to read *Slaughterhouse Five* and directed the English teacher to stop teaching the novel. The parent asked that all copies of *Slaughterhouse Five* be removed from the classroom and the school's library.

I first become aware of the concern regarding *Slaughterhouse Five* from the principal, who asked me if the library had a copy. I let him know the copy was checked out. The principal asked me to visit with him about the book. Later on I found the principal with two of the assistant principals in the break room taking their lunch. The principal asked me if I had read *Slaughterhouse Five,* and I said no. He then asked if I knew anything of a controversial nature about the book and showed me the drawing of swirly nipples and a necklace on pages toward the back of the book (I think that's where they were; I had difficulty clearly seeing naked breasts until they were pointed out to me). I was then told that a parent had complained about the naked drawing and numerous references to bestiality.

During this casual conversation about the book, which none of us had read, the assistant principal who handled the original complaint said several times to "pull it" from the library. I was told the English department chair and English teacher were told to pull it from the classroom. Before attending this casual meeting, and because the principal had asked about *Slaughterhouse Five* in particular, I had checked on any action the Supreme Court may have taken regarding this particular book. In fact, the Supreme Court had upheld First Amendment rights of high school students to have the option of checking out *Slaughterhouse Five* from the school library. As I conveyed this relevant information to the principal, the assistant principal was still piping up with "pull it." I asked the principal if I could take the evening to read the book and provide a reasoned opinion and recommendation to be available the following morning. The principal agreed and thanked me.

My assessment ran something like this: This novel is not a casual or fun read and would be well suited for a literature study project introduced by an experienced teacher who would provide balanced instruction in American themes and writers, American history, and the culture of war. Literature's purpose is to provide impressions of a period in time from various perspectives and through various types of writing. Vonnegut's narrative of his experience in Dresden, his suffering from post-traumatic shock as a prisoner of war (particularly removing dead bodies of civilians after Dresden was bombed), is accepted as a period piece—an antiwar protest piece in American literature. It was first published in 1969 during the counterculture movement and antiwar protest of Vietnam. It is also one person's perspective.

The mention of the pornographic picture three or four times (of which the parent was concerned) seems to be a way Vonnegut asserts that evil and immorality have existed from the beginning of recorded history. The picture is described through the narrator as the first pornographic daguerreotype. Vonnegut also mentions God raining down fierce judgment on people by destroying Sodom and Gomorrah. His rambling thoughts from first-person narrative to third-person narrative leave the reader to draw parallels of war as God's judgment: "fire and brimstone in the destruction of Sodom and Gomorrah" and "bombing of Dresden." Perhaps more disturbing than the mentions (not more than four, maybe three) of the "image" identified by a parent is the wildly disturbing mental rambling of the antihero, which is Vonnegut's way of dealing with his experience, his protest of all war. The tone is purposefully depressing, dehumanizing, and is the grinding nature of his protest. Vonnegut himself suffered from depression and once tried to kill himself.

Anyone reading this would agree that the destruction of human life is deplorable. The bombing of England was deplorable—an act of war. Students would be the first to observe that Germany started war with England.

Ultimately, I recommended that the book be recataloged into the non-fiction literature section (800s) under war literature. This removes it from the fiction section, which is heavily promoted. Removing the book from the library, I advised, is not in the school's best interest, particularly in the long run. Several issues are at stake. Mainly, the precedent would be established for anyone with an objection to any book to petition for its removal on the basis of their personal beliefs. Possible unwanted media attention is another aspect. The Supreme Court has ruled specifically on this particular title and its attempted removal from a public school library. Minors' First Amendment liberties include the right to receive information, as decided in *Board of Education v. Pico,* 457 U.S. 853 (1982).

This situation presented me an opportunity to provide professional advice to my principal and copartner in the library program, to work together to solve a problem. Our school district is conservative, and I realized the call to remove the book could go either way. I presented a solution that would appease the superintendent, principal, and parent while upholding the Constitution and guaranteeing any student access to *Slaughterhouse Five* from the library collection. The principal and superintendent agreed with my solution, and the book was not removed from the library collection. Students may locate *Slaughterhouse Five* in the library's catalog, check it out, and make their own decisions about liking or disliking the content.

What struck me during this situation was the idea that in a blink of an eye censorship can strike any library. If one book is removed, then others could follow. As a librarian and major stakeholder in what books are selected and deselected in the library, I knew that being prepared with information and given the chance to participate in a discussion about the concern offered me a way to solve the challenge issue. I believed this to be a true test of my worth as a librarian, to argue for the title to remain available to readers. I knew that my reasoning must be sound and that my opinion would need to be valued for the principal and administrator to stand behind my recommendation.

My degree in library and information science and subsequent classwork did cover challenges. Assignments in class presented scenarios that may occur in libraries, with recommendations on what to do when they happen. The American Library Association website offers tools for reference that are valuable, such as Supreme Court cases that uphold students' right to read *Slaughterhouse Five.* The opportunity to participate in a challenge was valuable in that I gained a better understanding of the levels of concern from teen reader, parent, English teacher, English department chair, principal, and superintendent. I do believe that the Supreme Court decisions had a direct impact on the principal's decision to agree with my recommendation.

CHAPTER 9

The Princess Librarian
An Allegory

SHERRY YORK

ONCE UPON a time in an imaginary land far, far away, there was born a beautiful, sweet, intelligent little princess who grew up to be a gorgeous, dynamic, perceptive woman who always wanted to be a librarian. After considerable travails and going down a variety of paths (but that's another story), she became a school librarian, and a damn good one at that. In fact, some people said she was the best librarian they had ever known. And she was!

She personified all that was good and true in the field of school librarianship. At the first school where she was librarian, she revamped the card catalog, weeded the collection, started a library club, sponsored a benefit dance to raise money for a scholarship to help a worthy student library aide go to college, worked well with students and teachers, and received high marks on her annual evaluations. Because she had learned that a selection policy is essential, she worked with the school administration to create such a policy. And it was good!

Somewhere along the way, she married a prince of a fellow who also became a school librarian. This librarian prince later turned into a frog, but that's another story. After some time had passed, the princess librarian and her husband decided that they should move to another district to be close to their aging parents. So they did.

That is how the princess librarian found herself working in a small, isolated, imaginary town where everyone knew everyone. And everyone in that town (well, almost everyone in that imaginary town) was sincere, hardworking, with the most impeccable intentions and always willing to help others. And that was interesting.

In that imaginary town there was no public library per se. One room of the high school library where the princess librarian was assigned was designated as the "adult library." The princess librarian was, amazingly, also the town's "public librarian." Sadly, the children's books that belonged to the "adult library" were kept packed away in the basement except in the summers, but that's another story.

The seniors in that high school were considered mature enough to handle "adult" material. So the seniors, during their study hall period (yes, the study halls met in the library, but that is also another story), were allowed to check out books from the adjacent "adult library" room. And some did.

One young man had a particular fondness for, of all things, the novels of Stephen King. In fact, this young man, who was not particularly scholarly, devoured several of that author's novels. And the princess librarian was glad.

As events later transpired, she learned that the young man's grandfather, with whom the young man lived, was also the president of the school board of that mythical school district. Once when the princess librarian met with the school board, the president of the school board questioned the princess librarian about how she went about purchasing books for the library. From his tone and demeanor (because she was so perceptive, discerning, and insightful) the princess librarian understood that he thought that she did not actually read much of anything and that she likely bought books only on subjects that interested her—things like cookbooks and needlepoint, perhaps. And she was chagrined.

Although she had been caught off guard, she answered succinctly in what she hoped was an inoffensive but convincing manner about selecting materials to meet the needs and interests of all who would be using the library for research and for pleasure reading. The president of the school board seemed unimpressed by the princess librarian's explanation but did not comment further. And she was apprehensive.

Later the superintendent of the mythical school explained that the president had been very concerned about the crude language he had seen in a book that his grandson had been reading. As it happened, the book in question had been checked out from the "adult library" because the young grandson was a senior that year. The princess librarian explained and the matter was dropped. And she was relieved.

The princess librarian was glad that she had the foresight to develop a selection policy, which the school administration and board had approved. Although she never experienced an official library materials challenge, she learned that most would-be censors were sincere in their concerns. And she grew wiser.

During her years in that mystical small town, she encountered books in which every "hell," "damn," and other mild expletive had been inked out, thus emphasizing said "hell," "damn," etc. And she was incensed.

While she labored on, teaching students about the library, she encountered many teachers (more than one) who had been ordained by God to monitor the content of all library books, but none of those saintly concerned individuals ever officially pursued a request for reconsideration of library materials. And the princess librarian muttered under her breath, but kept her own counsel.

When a new young high school principal confiscated *Crosses* by Shelly Stoehr, because someone at her church had made a comment to her about it, the princess librarian patiently explained the selection policy, the procedure for examination of library materials, and the necessity for a certain amount of realistic language and content in contemporary novels. The principal returned the library book and apologized for what she had done. Once again, the princess librarian triumphed. And she was both exasperated and relieved.

Eventually, when she worked with others to establish the first real public library in Make-Believe County, she had the privilege of training the new public librarian and was able to pass along her knowledge and philosophy. The princess librarian served on the board of the public library for several terms and watched proudly as the public librarian grew into a first-rate defender of patrons' right to read. And that was gratifying!

After the princess librarian had worked with several superintendents and school boards to develop a district-wide technology plan for libraries, she automated the high school library, conducted an in-house retrospective conversion of the library collection, saw the installation of a twenty-computer lab in the library, and proudly led in-service training to teach teachers about Boolean searching on the library's online catalog. She witnessed the advent of CD-ROM technology, CD-ROM encyclopedias and magazine article collections, and the Internet. The world of libraries and information had expanded, and she knew that in this new cyberworld librarians would face more questions and challenges. And it was beyond good. It was magical!

After she retired at a ridiculously young age, the princess librarian parted company with the prince frog and embarked with relish on a new enchanted path. She published a plethora of excellent, well-reviewed guide books on multicultural literature for librarians, became an editor helping other librarians write and publish books of their own, wrote an enthralling memoir, became leader of a book discussion group, and presented stirring inspirational programs at library conferences in several states. When the Harry Potter books were publicly burned in a nearby anonymous town, she realized that censorship still existed. And she was saddened.

The princess librarian was last seen checking out books from the local public library and buying books from thrift stores. Some of the books she reads contain really bad language, even an occasional f-word. Gasp! A while back she created a catalog of donated books for her writers' group using her laptop computer. She is currently waiting for responses to her recent newspaper ad seeking someone to dust and organize the books in her extensive private collection. As you may have guessed, the princess librarian is living happily ever after!

CHAPTER 10

The Complexity and Challenges of Censorship in Public Schools

Overstepping Boundaries, Cultivating Compassionate Conversations

MARIE-ELISE WHEATWIND

I HAVE always loved starting off the school year reading banned books, as did most of my students and their parents. During back-to-school night, or during end-of-the-year conferences for my Gifted and Talented Education (GATE) and honors courses, they often mentioned this assignment and enthusiastically spoke about how much they enjoyed discussing a book they hadn't realized was challenged or censored. For other parents and students, the assignment was praised for getting students interested in reading, and by students as introducing them to the first book they "had to read for school" that they really enjoyed.

I created the unit as an autonomous reading assignment. It required that each student select a book from a list. Each student signed up for a different book so they could report on it in oral presentations to their classmates. The main restrictions were that the book had to be grade or age appropriate and subject to both parent's and teacher's signed approval. For GATE students, these guidelines weren't much of a hindrance, for many of them were already reading at a college level. When I adapted the assignment to teach to general ninth-grade readers, the "age appropriate" requirement was harder to gauge. I saw a wider range of reading and writing abilities because students filtered into high school from different middle schools, charter schools, and homeschool situations. I used the American Library Association's extensive materials, including the ALA definition of intellectual freedom and an annotated list of books that have been challenged and banned, which ALA updates every year.[1] Because I wanted to be respectful of the families' different religious, philosophical, and political sensibilities, information and permission forms were sent home so the students and parents could peruse the lists and discuss which books might be the most appropriate for their individual needs.

The reading was to be done outside of class, as well as during silent sustained reading (SSR) in class (usually twice a week for twenty minutes). Other requirements included a brief written overview about the book's plot, themes, and characters due during the first week of reading, along with some research about where and why the book had been challenged or censored. Small group discussions occurred in the weeks following, with each student presenting from a reading log their arguments or reflections about why they agreed or disagreed with the book's censorship, either for people of their own age or for younger readers. A final presentation or final paper, which synthesized all of these components, sometimes included a poster display or larger class discussion. Usually after the unit ended, momentum continued among many students independently, with the reading of one another's papers and swapping of books.

Because school-wide SSR was not implemented in every school in which I taught, over the years I developed my own SSR classroom library, eventually amassing more than one hundred books. Many of the titles in the collection were on the ALA banned book list. These boxes of books traveled with me from school to school during my teaching career, and when favorites were borrowed and not returned I replaced them with used copies, especially if they were not available in the school library. Fortunately, I did not have to worry about a paucity of books when I began teaching at Tucson (Arizona) High Magnet School in 2007. The school's head librarian, Amy Rusk, showed up at our first English department faculty meeting in August, inviting us to contribute titles and suggestions of books and materials. She provided a sign-up sheet so we could schedule classes in the library in September and October to view a banned book display and hear her lecture about censorship and First Amendment rights.[2]

I started my banned book unit in the fall semester the same week that my ninth-grade English classes visited the library and examined the many books in Rusk's display. Students were incensed to learn that some of their childhood favorites (*Where's Waldo, In the Night Kitchen, Charlie and the Chocolate Factory*) had been challenged or removed from public and school libraries. As anticipated, the displayed books attracted their interest, with very few students claiming they "couldn't find anything to read" for the assignment. When I suspected some students of attempting to fulfill the assignment with a book they had read previously, I would remind them that they had to bring back a signed parent and teacher approval form. This often prompted classmates to recommend favorites they had read. One pair of friends, John and Joey, had each been reprimanded by the principal for lunchtime fighting and inappropriate cell phone use in classes. They were examining the cover of Anthony Burgess's *A Clockwork Orange.* This title was not included on my recommended list, nor was it part of my SSR library. John, who had seen the movie, encouraged Joey to choose it as his book before someone else signed up for it. Knowing the age-level and grade-level reading disparity of both boys, I suggested that Joey read the first few pages before checking it out of the library, warning him that he might find its cockney dialect confusing and hard to follow. When I reminded him that his mother also had to approve the book, he retorted, "She'll sign the paper; she just wants to see me reading, she don't care what it is."

Another student, Jane, approached me after the bell rang. She had seen Anne Rice's *Interview with a Vampire* on my list, but it had already been checked out of the library, and the book was missing from my SSR shelves. She told me her mom had all of Rice's books at home; I asked if she had already read any of them herself. Confessing that she had read *Interview,* she asked to read the second in the series, *The Vampire Lestat,* which wasn't on my recommended list. Already aware of her reading level and maturity, I said I would approve her reading that title, but only if her mother agreed as well.

Within a few days, most of the signed permission slips had been re-turned, with many students bringing their books to school so they could read them during SSR. When I noticed Joey flipping through a graphic novel that first week, I warned him that if he didn't turn in his written assignment on time I would call his mom and suggest that he choose a different book. I noticed that Jane also read from other books in my class-room library during SSR, but after she told me her mother preferred that she not take any of Rice's books out of their house, I didn't give it another thought.

A phone call to Joey's mother was prompted days later by his being caught fighting again. As we talked about homework assignments he would have to complete while serving in-school detention, I mentioned my heightened concern about his reading *A Clockwork Orange,* which contained many depictions of violence and a brutal rape scene. She admitted that she had signed the book contract without discussing her son's book choice and questioned why I would assign it to a ninth-grader if I felt it might not be appropriate for him to read. I responded by citing the district policy: "When a book is taken into the classroom by a teacher it becomes 'curriculum' and is much more vulnerable to scrutiny, but a student has a 'right to read' and choose from a library what he or she wants."[3] I reminded Joey's mother that the assignment required the informed approval by a parent as well as me, and that I had cautioned him about the book's language.

"Oh, he likes the language, all right," she replied, "and he wants me to rent the movie too." I discouraged this, for I was afraid it would compromise the time Joey spent reading and influence his writing. She asked if I had seen the movie and if I had ever shown it in my classes.

"Yes, I saw it while in college and found it very disturbing," I answered honestly. "I would never show it in a high school classroom, because of its R rating [restricted: under 17 must be accompanied by a parent or guardian]."

"Well then, that settles it," she said. "I don't allow him to watch R-rated movies, so he'll have to choose a different book. I don't mind about the language. He hears it all the time at school and on the street. But the excessive violence is too much."

Joey was angry and disappointed when I brought a few alternative banned book choices to him in detention. He eventually completed the assignment by reading S. E. Hinton's *The Outsiders,* which he admitted was the first "whole book" he had ever read outside of class "cover to cover," because he "could relate" to what it was about.

Meanwhile, after a series of sporadic absences, Jane handed in her first written banned book assignment almost three weeks late. When I settled down to read and grade it during prep, I discovered that the "awesome" book she was reading was not the agreed-upon *Vampire Lestat* but a novel written by Anne Rice under the pseudonym A. N. Roquelaure, titled *The Claiming of Sleeping Beauty.* I double-checked her book contract, making sure that this title was not what corresponded with Jane's and her mother's signature, and pulled her out of her last class to discuss this in the hallway.

"You said you didn't want me to read anything I'd read before, and I actually read *The Vampire Lestat* last summer," she said defiantly. "My mom knows I'm reading this book instead. Go ahead and call her." I pointed out that her contract misrepresented her mother's consent as well as her original intention and circumvented my permission, which I would not give for this assignment. I assumed I wouldn't have any trouble reasoning with Jane's mother about this book—which I knew was labeled as "erotica" as well as "pornography" and was not included in the high school library.

I assumed incorrectly. Jane's mother told me tersely that her fourteen-year-old daughter had "been around the block" and could read whatever she wanted, including books that depicted graphic sexual relationships, because that was something that they were very open about. She offered to sign a different contract with Roquelaure's title on it. "We've been talking about it when I drive her to school in the morning," she said. "It's been great. If you tell her she can't read it for your out-of-class assignment, then she'll want to read it all the more on her own, and I'm fine with that." She laughed, adding, "Isn't this whole thing about censorship? I'm not going to censor my daughter's reading, even if that's what you seem intent on doing."

"Whatever Jane reads outside of class is her business," I replied, "but she'll have to choose a different book to read for this particular assignment, because it involves small group discussions with her classmates; most of them are, like your daughter, only fourteen years old." I thought about a young refugee from Afghanistan, who wore a head scarf and spoke about some of her Muslim beliefs in class one day. I knew that other Christian students—both boys and girls—attended a weekly lunch meeting to discuss the Bible. I doubted that any of these students' parents were as open about sexuality as Jane and her mother were, and that the focus of our classroom discussions might be derailed if Jane began describing the sexual details of her book rather than addressing the facts of its censorship.

"If Jane switches books now, she'll get behind in your class, and that will hurt her grade," her mother argued further.

"Her grade will be compromised even more if I refuse to let her discuss this book in class, nor could she do a final presentation on it. I hope you will at least agree with me that this is not a book that is appropriate for most ninth-graders to read or discuss," I countered. "If I'd known three weeks ago that she intended to read Roquelaure instead of Rice, I would have steered her toward other choices sooner because it is not within the original parameters of the assignment." As I spoke with Jane's mom, I was confident that the high school principal, Abel Morado, would back me up if our conversation couldn't be resolved over the phone.

Jane's mother continued, "I'm assuming that you've actually *read* Anne Rice's books?"

"I've read the vampire series," I answered, "but not any of the Roquelaure novels. From what I know about them, I doubt that I would ever choose to read them."

"So you're actually doing what most censors do! You're basing your opinion of this book on what you've heard—possibly out of context—instead of on what you know firsthand." Before I could respond, she hung up the phone.

I didn't have to wait long to discuss this with Jane. She stopped by my classroom after school, following a cell phone conversation with her mother. I told her she had not followed the generous boundaries of the assignment (made even more flexible by my allowing her to read a book that wasn't included on the original list of recommended titles). I then emphasized that it would affect her grade if she didn't choose a different book to discuss in a small group as well as write about in her final paper, as I would not allow her the option of a class presentation. I also suggested that she and her mother were welcome to meet with Principal Morado and me at their earliest convenience for any further discussion.

In a normal teaching year, that would have been the end of it. I would have held my ground, arguing that what little reading time Jane had should be spent reading literature that would prepare her for more advanced classes, tests, and college. But what Jane didn't know was that this would be my last year of teaching. I had been accepted into the University of Arizona's School of Information Resource and Library Science graduate program and was looking forward to a new career as a librarian. If Jane's mother was poised to challenge me about her daughter's reading, even though I felt confident that my job would not be in jeopardy, I also felt an inner challenge: I wanted to be able to present an informed opinion about why the writings of Roquelaure were not appropriate for a high school reader. I imagined those morning conversations between Jane and her mother on the way to school. What other perspectives about the fantasy of an idealized, erotic relationship would she hear, other than the ones she might share with friends, or see depicted in movies, on billboards, and in magazines?

Jane returned to my classroom during lunch and after school a few more times in the days that followed, sometimes alone, other times with her best friend. As often happens when students sit and work on homework or overdue assignments, I listened to the chatter about their lives. Unlike many girls her age, Jane had an enviable close bond with her mother. Because she was treated more like a sister or friend than a daughter, Jane disapproved of her divorced mother's choice of boyfriends and felt that her own boyfriend (a classmate) treated her more respectfully than the men her mother dated.

As Jane continued to argue with me about finishing Roquelaure's novel, she also begged me to read it, so that she could prove me wrong about my "judgment" of its contents. She pointed out that in other classes students or their parents could request that an alternative assignment be given if they thought the book's story might be emotionally upsetting. This had occurred in my sophomore class when a student and her family requested that she read something other than *The Kite Runner,* for she didn't want to be a part of any discussions about the witnessed rape scene.

My conversations with Jane about *The Claiming of Sleeping Beauty* began when she showed up alone and listless after school, and soon after that her mother called to confirm that we had been discussing Roquelaure's novel. When her mother asked me if I would make a special case for Jane and allow our private discussions to "count" toward Jane's grade instead of her participating in group discussions, I agreed. At this point Jane's poor school attendance was affecting her grades in all of her classes. More important, my own reading of the novel made me hope I could offer Jane a feminist interpretation of the book that might help her see its contents in a different light. This was not easy.

Although Roquelaure's modern retelling of *Sleeping Beauty* takes place in medieval times and involves a prince awakening a sleeping princess, it is clear from the beginning that the expanded story provides a platform for descriptions of sexual fantasies of slavery and submission. Jane did not initially see anything wrong with this, for she felt that the young princess was "in love" with the prince. She felt the princess's submission to him was a way of showing her obedience and depth of feelings, perhaps like Jane's own recently awakened feelings toward her boyfriend, with whom she revealed she was sexually involved. When I initially tried to focus our discussion on the reasons why Roquelaure's novel might be considered inappropriate for most adolescents, she was quick to point out that in other countries (and, in fact, in some states of our nation) various laws allowed girls her age to marry, making their sexual activity "legal and respectable." I asked her to think about whom these laws might benefit most, especially in countries where poor parents allowed girls to be "married" at ages much younger than fourteen. Her response was that in other countries this was all accepted as part of their culture. I asked her how many cultures allow women to have more than one husband, and if she thought she would like to live in a culture where her "marriage" would be arranged at a very young age, without her consent or control over who her husband might be.

What ultimately turned our discussion toward the issue of censorship and the appropriateness of Roquelaure's writing was my asking her to consider the innocence and naivete of some of her classmates—both male and female. I could see her resisting this at first, perhaps because she thought that, regardless of their experience, they knew all about sex. I asked her to imagine reading this book aloud to a young child of five or six who, having heard a lot of fairy tales, was begging for something new, something she hadn't heard before.

"She wouldn't understand it," Jane interrupted. "She doesn't need to hear about that stuff at such a young age."

"What if a parent wanted to read this to that child and the parent helped her to understand it?" She became quiet as I continued: "Some of the parents of your classmates moved here from other countries so that their children wouldn't have to grow up too fast. Those parents want their children to remain children, and remain in school longer than they might have been able to in the countries they moved from. Some of those parents, who may have never finished school themselves, want more choices for their girls than marriage to someone they love at a young age, followed by a life of poverty and hard work. They want their girls to go to college, to live fulfilling lives."

Our conversation about Roquelaure's novel ended with that discussion, as did my reading of the book. I was able to steer Jane toward other books and suggested that she encourage her mother to read some of them with her. I have often thought about the choice I made during that final teaching of censorship, and wonder why I did it. I realize that in doing so, I may have put my job more in jeopardy than if I had held to the parameters of the assignment. But I am satisfied that the arguments I was able to make to Jane in our conversations were respected, not because I had compromised but because I had found a means to expand her way of valuing and understanding the innocent child she no longer chose to be. Perhaps her compassion for others also helped her to nurture some compassion for herself as well.

NOTES

1. American Library Association, "Intellectual Freedom," www.ala.org/ala/issues advocacy/intfreedom/index.cfm
2. Amy Rusk also serves as the cochair (along with Christy Friske-Daniels) of the Tucson Unified School District Library Resource Review Committee.
3. Amy Rusk clarified the school district policy in an e-mail to me dated March 12, 2010.

PART III

Not Only Boy Scouts Should Be Prepared

Building Strong Policies

Did you ever hear anyone say, "That work had better be banned because I might read it and it might be very damaging to me?"
—JOSEPH HENRY JACKSON

POLICIES are time-consuming and sometimes painful documents to write, but, when librarians encounter challenges to material in their library's holdings or are accused of censorship, these documents may shine like the most beautiful pieces of gold ever discovered. Librarians must have collection development policies and materials reconsideration policies to protect themselves and the communities they serve from people who want material removed from the library. A well-written collection development policy and reconsideration policy set the stage for librarians and concerned patrons. These policies explain each participant's role in the conversation and how the story is to move forward toward its eventual conclusion. Policies are the first step and the first guide toward providing a thoughtful and clear response to any question a patron may have about a book or movie in the library's collection.

CHAPTER 11

I Owe It All to Madonna

LISË CHLEBANOWSKI

IN 1992, the year that Madonna published her book *Sex,* I was a part-time library clerk at the Downers Grove Public Library in Downers Grove, Illinois. I had no aspirations whatsoever to be a librarian. It was just a nice job with hours that were convenient for someone with young children. The Downers Grove Public Library had a written policy regarding collection development, and Madonna's book fit the criteria for purchase: more than five requests, a place on the top ten *New York Times* best-seller list, and of pop culture interest. One copy was purchased and soon the reserve cards poured in, but soon so did the request for reconsideration forms. I was among the dozen or so patrons who had filled out reservation cards, and so I was surprised that there was an issue with the book. I was simply a part-time clerk with little knowledge of censorship and even less knowledge of professional librarianship.

Within a few days, the book had been taken off the display and put in the director's office until further notice, awaiting the library board's decision. The people who filled out the request forms did not think the book was appropriate for our other patrons or their children. Of course, I was stunned. "Who do they think they are?" I asked. "What gives them the right to decide what I can and can't read?" I was outraged, passionate, and, most of all, determined. I went to the office of the library director and timidly knocked on his door. I told him that I felt the book belonged in the library, no matter how repugnant it might be. I told him I wanted to help in any way I could. He obliged my request with a list of names and phone numbers of some of the most ardent library supporters. "Call them," he said. "They will help you." Well, did they ever! Together we formed the Downers Grove Library Advocates, more than eighty members strong, to defend this book against its many detractors.

Both sides were passionate in their defense of their beliefs, and law enforcement was a visible presence at each hearing. After more than a year and several vocal and contentious public hearings, the library board voted to retain the book. The detractors of the book tried everything to convince the board otherwise. They suggested the book be kept behind a desk available by request; they suggested the book was pornographic and obscene; they "knew" the book would not last (its spiral binding would not tolerate more than one or two circulations); and they demanded the town relinquish control of the library and convert it, at great taxpayer expense, to a district library. In the end, the book was retained. It circulated to more than one hundred holds and then circulated to almost as many interlibrary loan requests, until one day it simply fell apart.

By the time the book self-destructed, I had an intellectual freedom award hanging on my wall and was well on my way to a master's degree in library science. Who would have thought that this book would be such a career catalyst? Although I have fought several subsequent challenges, I like to say that I owe it all to Madonna.

CHAPTER 12

The Battle to Include

GRETCHEN GOULD

IN THE spring of 2009, the head of collection management and special services (CMSS) at my library informed me that we had received a request to subscribe to an academic journal in print.[1] In addition, the requestor, a campus community member, had offered to pay for an institutional subscription. Because I was the bibliographer for political science, this journal—*Occidental Quarterly: Western Perspectives on Man, Culture and Politics* (*TOQ*)—fell within my subject area. I started browsing the print issues that had been provided to us by the campus community member as well as the journal's website.

We started the review process by using the standard set of criteria and collection management tools we use for all academic journals. We checked standard periodical guides as well as general and subject-specific periodical indexes and abstracts our patrons use to identify articles of potential interest and did not find *TOQ* listed. We performed some searches in JSTOR and did not find any reviews of *TOQ*. We also checked in WorldCat and found that five libraries subscribed to this journal and only two libraries appeared to have current subscriptions. Only three academic libraries had subscriptions to *TOQ*. This, to me, was an indicator that *TOQ* was not a scholarly journal in the field of political science. If it were a legitimate scholarly journal, it would be carried by hundreds, if not thousands, of academic libraries and would be well known. Another area of concern was identifying the publisher, which ended up being a challenging process. When I looked for specific information about the publisher, I found different locations listed, only post office box addresses, and no phone numbers. The only way to contact *TOQ* was through e-mail or sending something to a post office box. This was another indicator to me that this journal did not meet scholarly standards.

We went above and beyond our normal review process by looking at the authors and articles published in *TOQ*. We checked several databases to see if any of the articles or authors had been reviewed. Some of the authors had published in other scholarly journals, and those articles had been reviewed, but none of the articles in *TOQ* had ever been reviewed. This raised a red flag in my mind as to the journal's credibility.

We went even further by reviewing a selection of specific articles that had been published in *TOQ*. In this review, we also examined the footnotes. It became apparent to me that these articles would not be considered scholarly. The articles had incomplete footnote citations, no references listed, and biased and unreliable sources such as Fox News and Wikipedia listed. The articles that were online on the *TOQ* website appeared to have no citations or footnotes.

The final step we took in the review process was examining the actual content of the material written. It became clear to me quickly that the articles in *TOQ* contained material that would be considered offensive. For example, one of the articles started off with "Prepare to fight to the finish, or your kind will vanish." In the first paragraph of the same article, the author wrote, "In the last two years, one crisis has followed another . . . involving a crisis of the spirit which brought a negro to power—a negro symbolizing everything against which the American originally defined himself, and thus symbolizing the destruction of America's historic identity."[2] I could not believe the term *negro,* outdated and considered offensive to many, was still being used.

The head of CMSS and I met and discussed the information we had gathered during the review process. First and foremost, we decided not to subscribe to *TOQ* because it did not appear to meet the definition of a scholarly academic journal. Secondarily, we felt that this journal did not express ideas and thoughts in a constructive, scholarly manner.

The CMSS head contacted the campus community member and stated our decision to decline the offer of an institutional subscription to *TOQ*. She explained the review process and the established selection criteria we used to reach our decision. She indicated that the library strived to provide access to a broad range of viewpoints but that we found the views expressed frequently in *TOQ* not in keeping with the diversity-related goals of the university.[3] She pointed out that the library provided access to other journals, in both print and electronic format, that expressed a range of conservative perspectives, such as *American Conservative* and *National Review.* She also pointed out that most, if not all, of the full text of *TOQ* issues was available free of charge and restriction through the journal's website. At this point, I thought the situation had been resolved.

We received a prompt response in which the campus community member rebutted our assessment that views expressed frequently in *TOQ* were not in keeping with the diversity-related goals of the university. The member noted that the library owned a copy of Daniel Jonah Goldhagen's *Hitler's Willing Executioners: Ordinary Germans and the Holocaust,* which he felt contained materials far more questionable than anything in *TOQ* and thus should be removed from the library shelves. If we chose not to remove Goldhagen's book from the library collection, we were to tell him why. In his judgment, our concerns were inconsistent with the central purpose of a university. He indicated that he was willing to identify objectionable statements in Goldhagen's book if we desired, and he respectfully asked if there was an appeals process and what the specific procedures entailed.

I remember being slightly taken aback; I had not expected this kind of response. I thought we had made an informed decision utilizing the established selection criteria and all of the collection management tools available to us. In fact, because there was so little information, we went further in researching *TOQ* than we might have otherwise done for an academic journal.

The head of CMSS responded to the campus community member, explaining that there were procedures for handling challenges to include or exclude materials in the library collection. The member should submit his challenges in writing. The challenges would then be reviewed with consideration given to diverse viewpoints being represented. It is the policy of the library that we do not add or withdraw, at the request of any individual or group, materials that have been chosen or excluded on the basis of established selection criteria. If the campus community member wished to challenge the library's decision not to accept the gift institutional subscription to *TOQ,* documentation as to why the journal should be made available in print in the library was required. If he wished to challenge the inclusion of Goldhagen's book, he needed to provide evidence to support that position.

I thought this was simple and straightforward enough that the individual would submit his challenges to include *TOQ* in print and exclude Goldhagen's book. Instead, he responded with his philosophy on the First Amendment and what happened when people like Hitler and Stalin told people what they could or could not read. He wanted the head of CMSS and I to provide him with specific statements from *TOQ* that led to our decision. He would then respond by providing us with information from sources within the library that could be compared with statements from *TOQ.* Only with this procedure, the campus community member felt, could he use our time appropriately to resolve what he believed merited attention in a free society. He thanked us for our interest in a high-quality education upon which an authentic democracy depended.

I started becoming frustrated that a simple, straightforward process had turned into a philosophical argument that would just keeping going around in the same circles. The head of CMSS and I decided not to address any of the specific statements and simply reiterated that the next step in the process was for the requestor to provide a statement explaining why he thought issues of *TOQ* should be made available in print. He responded and wanted to present evidence that none of the content in *TOQ* exceeded general American views any more than some of the books in our library. He stated that he did not want to present problems but that for judgments to be made, comparisons should be implemented. Again, the head of CMSS and I decided not to address any of the specific statements in the response and informed him that he could include additional information in his statement addressing why print issues of *TOQ* should be made available in the library.

The next communication we received from the campus community member stated that he had talked to several people about how he should handle this matter. The people he had consulted had recommended that fairness be applied to the situation. He felt that judgments had been made about the content of *TOQ* and that those judgments must have been based on specific printed statements in *TOQ*. He then requested that the head of CMSS and I provide him with those allegedly inappropriate statements from *TOQ*. He, in turn, would then provide us with material that was available in the library and had similar inappropriateness. He stated that he had begun gathering such information and, in the process, decided that he should not have to pay to have *TOQ* in the library; the library should set aside funds for such equitable access to information. He apologized for the complications but wanted this to be settled fairly and equitably. He requested that, due to the sensitivity of the topic, our communications with him be confidential. That struck me: he thought it was perfectly okay to talk to other people about this situation, yet he expected us to keep the information confidential. We did so, anyhow, because it is one of the core principles of librarianship.

We responded by indicating that we would not be initiating a paid subscription to *TOQ*. We reiterated the fact that *TOQ* was not listed in the standard periodical guides, nor was it covered by either general or subject-specific periodical indexes or abstracts that would be used to identify articles of potential interest. We restated that the library provided access to other political science journals, in print and electronic format, that covered a range of conservative perspectives. We named some specific journals, such as *National Review* and *Weekly Standard*. Finally, we emphasized that a majority of the content from the issues of *TOQ* was available free of charge and restriction through the journal's website. The library was not blocking or restricting access to the journal's website. We reaffirmed our decision not to add the print subscription of *TOQ* to the library collection.

Yet again we were asked to identify three specific statements from *TOQ* that led to the decision that the contents were inconsistent with the prevalent diversity emphasis at our university. He could then compare our three statements with specific statements or materials in the library, presumably paid for by tax dollars, that violated what was considered diversity. He felt that we should implement policies at the library consistent with what people expected from a university library.

At the same time the head of CMSS contacted the library dean about how to respond to this campus community member, the campus community member also contacted the library dean. The library dean supported the decision made by the head of CMSS and me. She also consulted with members of the university administration, including the university legal counsel, about this situation. A meeting was held with the university administrators, the library dean, and the head of CMSS regarding this situation and how to proceed. The university administration reviewed our communications with the campus community member, supported our decision not to subscribe to *TOQ* in print, and helped craft a response to the campus community member. It was decided that any further complaints would be addressed by members of the university administration.

The head of CMSS wrote one final e-mail to the campus community member in which she reiterated, yet again, that the criteria used to evaluate *TOQ* was the same criteria used to evaluate all other journals. She restated that the primary reason for our decision was not the fact that views in *TOQ* were not in keeping with the diversity-related goals of the university. She specifically recapped all of the reasons we decided not to subscribe to *TOQ*, indicated that she would not be supplying any specific examples, and stated that the decision was final and that she would not respond to further communication on the request.

This issue has been resolved with the university administration, and the campus community member has agreed not to pursue this matter further. The situation was a huge learning experience for me. The one thing I could never understand was why the campus community member was so insistent on having the library subscribe to this journal in print. Most of the material from the journal was free on the journal's website, and the library did not put any restrictions on accessing the journal's website. If the library had been restricting access to the journal's website as well as refusing to subscribe to the journal in print, I can see where one might have thought the library was censoring information.

Another thing that stood out in my mind was that the campus community member seemed unwilling to accept the fact that we had applied the same established set of criteria to this journal as we have done with all of the other academic journals we subscribe to.

This situation shed light on the fine line between selection and censorship. We chose not to subscribe to this journal on the basis of selection criteria, whereas the campus community member saw our decision as censorship. It was interesting to see the different interpretations and perspectives on this situation. After all that has been said and done in this matter, I am comfortable with our decision and stand by it. I feel we compiled objective information to support our decision and were not censoring. Still, as was evident in this case, people do not always see eye to eye.

NOTES

1. To maintain confidentiality, I generalize details and do not use personal names. The content of this chapter was taken from verbal and written communications among the parties involved.

2. Michael O'Meara, "2009: Crisis or Opportunity?" *Occidental Quarterly* 9 (2009): 1, www.toqonline.com/archives/v9n1/TOQv9n10Meara.pdf

3. University of Northern Iowa, "Diversity Definition, Vision and Mission," www.uni .edu/diversity/definition.shtml

CHAPTER 13

Pornography and Erotica in the Academic Library

MICHELLE MARTINEZ

From the pornographic imagination flow some of the most important tributaries of American Culture.

—JOSPEH W. SLADE, *Pornography and Sexual Representation*

MY UNIVERSITY and its library are in a small, conservative Texas town, and I ordered Guillaume Apollinaire's *Eleven Thousand Rods*. I am the library's English/literature bibliographer. I order books for the collection upon request of the faculty and based on what I believe will best serve the university and students. The modern glossy cover for the book explains much: "The uncensored erotic classic." And on the back it warns "explicit content." I purchased the book because it filled a gap in our collection of Apollinaire's material.

The book was handed back to me by the assistant director, who had received it covered in yellow sticky notes by a nontraditional student who marked the so-called naughty passages. My initial response was that the patron didn't read the book or else there would be no text unmarked. I was asked to defend my purchase by the assistant director in case she had to speak to the patron again.

Because I feel personally invested in my collection area, this seemed like a personal attack. I complained to my colleagues, and they commiserated with me, even becoming outraged that the book was challenged. Finally, I sat down to provide the assistant director with a good defense of the book should she need to deal with this again, or should the patron require further information. This is what I wrote:

I did some research on Apollinaire's *Eleven Thousand Rods* so that we could effectively address the patron's issues and be prepared to handle future inquiries of this nature. Libraries at Berkley, A&M, SFA, Rice, and Harvard also have this same book in their collection according to OCLC.

To begin with, there are warnings on the book cover: one on the front and one on the back warning of explicit material. Furthermore, had the patron read the introduction he would have been given a full explanation of the purpose of *Eleven Thousand Rods*.

Apollinaire was a major 20th century French poet who contributed widely to the avant-garde movements of the day such as Cubism. Apollinaire wrote two books of fiction, one of which was *Eleven Thousand Rods*.

Eleven Thousand Rods was meant to be shocking. It was intended to upset the censors. *ETR* was further an artistic attempt to stretch what was considered appropriate and distort it: what Apollinaire was doing with words, Cubists were doing with art. It was parallel.

As for supporting the curriculum, a wide variety of students and faculty members could use this book at any time during their studies. It's not just my goal to support what is currently being taught but to also look ahead and provide what may be taught. Erotica is becoming more mainstream as years pass and pornography has always been a topic of interest in the news, so it would not surprise me if students or faculty eventually demand a class that looks at this topic.

As for *currently* supporting the curriculum, students of French may want to look at a translation of a prominent and important French poet's work. *ETR* is unrevised in this edition for the first time, and wholly uncensored. Poetry students may wish to view this work as well as those students in English that are working in areas of the 20th century or world literature. Students taking classes in history, art, sociology, psychology, and human sexuality may find use of this particular text. *ETR* can be used in myriad ways—to look at the social mores of the time, to understand censorship, to learn how human sexuality was represented in the 20th century, to see an example of Cubism in words, to learn about what was considered pornography at the time but has since been dubbed erotica, to read a work in Apollinaire's *oeuvre,* or simply to read it.

I believe that having a collection that is merely selective based on less offensive material in the literary world would do the collection an injustice. The collection ought to not only support the current curriculum but should be allowed to grow to fill in gaps such as missing authors and missing works, including erotic fiction. Even if it is not specifically being taught, there is always a possible need and use for it.

There are many books in our collection that this patron may have found offensive such as almost anything by De Sade or Aristophanes' *Lysistrata* or Shakespeare's *Taming of the Shrew*. It is very important to integrate faculty input into collection development and we should also consider the needs of our students when determining what goes into our collection. However, we would be setting a dangerous precedent if patrons were given authority in collection development decisions. If we agree this particular work is pornography then soon we'll be pulling books such as Wilde's *The Picture of Dorian Gray* and Ginsberg's *Howl*.

I think it's best if the book remains in the collection and on the shelf where it can be found by library-users who may wish to read this book for whatever reasons, but I've checked it out for the moment—as soon as it returns it can go in its place.

Eleven Thousand Rods filled the library's gap in Apollinaire's collection. We have more than twenty of his titles, as my director reminded me in thanking me for my e-mail.

Curious about what would happen to the book, I found the library's collection development policy guidelines. The only mention of censorship in the policy guidelines refers to the reference collection: "There shall be no censorship of library resources, print or electronic." There is no written policy regarding the main collection where the Apollinaire book was located. Nor is there any written policy or procedures on how to handle challenged material. We don't have many challenges because we are an academic library, and most people expect to find a wide array of materials available, which is why, as the assistant director has pointed out, one of the most important policies we have is limiting children's access to the materials in the library.

When I spoke with the library director regarding the title, she said she would remove the book from the circulating collection and place it in the rare book room with the criminal justice material. Nothing circulates in the rare book room, and placing it with criminal justice material would potentially add further difficulty in finding the book. Furthermore, people browsing Apollinaire's work in the circulating collection wouldn't come across the title. From what was implied in our conversation, the director didn't agree with the objecting student's view nor did she like the possible solution; she just didn't want there to be library turmoil if it could be avoided.

My colleagues were bothered by the pending decision and urged me to follow up on this situation. At this time the book was still available for checkout, so I checked it out to read, informing my director I was doing so. Since I purchased the book and was asked to defend it, I wanted to be able to defend not just my decision but the content of the book, because I felt so personally about the situation. I wanted to be able to save the book for the circulating collection. Checking the book out had the added benefit that, once it was returned to the library, the issue would have cooled down and I could intelligently discuss the content with the director and address any further issues if the student returned to follow up on his complaint.

The book was checked out to me for a full semester (since I'm faculty) and was returned before the semester due date. The director allowed the book to return with the rest of our collection of Apollinaire. When I spoke with my director about the book after the incident, she said because the book was a slender volume she hoped it would slide between the larger volumes on the shelf and be forgotten or overlooked by potential complainants. At this point I realized that the book would remain there with the rest of the collection. I told my director how grateful I was that she had decided to let the book return to the shelf, to which she replied that she supported ALA and didn't believe in banning books, believing that if someone doesn't like a book, then they simply shouldn't read it.

This experience definitely changed me. I became an advocate for collecting sexually explicit materials. I don't force explicit materials into the collection, and I don't confuse censorship with the necessity of making choices based on economic constraints, but I'm better prepared to address any concerns or attempts at censorship when I do order books like the erotic version of *Pride and Prejudice.* I also became aware of the need for collection development policies and procedures regarding challenged materials. Furthermore, I learned that library directors are often caught in the cross fire when it comes to challenges: between the librarian and an angry patron over a challenged book.

I want to keep my job as much as the next librarian and I want to achieve tenure. Regardless, the purpose of erotica and pornography in my library, in the collection areas of which I am in charge, is to present a full collection of literature including the more "offensive" areas. I am there to serve the purpose as literature bibliographer and ensure that the students, faculty, and those patrons our campus serves have access to as full a collection of literature as possible.

I also decided to focus my areas of research in pornography and erotica when possible. I have since worked on papers with my colleague, Tyler Manolovitz, dealing with the sexually explicit, which include "Incest, Sexual Violence, and Rape in Video Games" (to be published in the *Video-game Cultures and the Future of Interactive Entertainment* e-journal), and presented papers and led discussions about censorship and pornography at conferences. I'm still nervous at times when I'm by myself and discussing a hot topic to a crowd of people I don't know.

My mother, when the challenge of the book came about, asked if I was really willing to make this a cause of mine, to argue against censorship. After all, I might be risking my job or lose the possibility of tenure, which is several years away still. I immediately said, "Yes. I'm willing to fight for this." She wasn't thrilled, but I remember her telling me that she was proud of me anyway.

I've discovered that a lot of people are on my side, from family (and, surprisingly, my grandmother and religious conservative cousins) to friends, coworkers, librarians, and authors. Perhaps my cousins, and those conservative-minded folks I've encountered, understand my argument, because I explain that to be against something and speak against it we have to know what exactly "it" is, which means identifying and collecting it (the sexually explicit material or whatever "it" may be for you).

I began researching collection development guidelines regarding sexually explicit materials and discovered that few libraries readily addressed this topic. Many libraries do collect explicit books by accident, without awareness of the sexual content. Some libraries have books now considered "literature," such as *Sons and Lovers* by D. H. Lawrence, or nonthreatening books such as art or anatomy texts. There are few universities that could be granted a flashing neon sign that says "Sexually Explicit Books Here!" because their campus libraries prefer not to draw attention to sexually explicit books when they do order them lest there be trouble—either patron complaints or theft of the books.

I also began reading all I could regarding collection development and sexually explicit materials. I didn't find much, particularly much that is recent. The entire time I dealt with defending the Apollinaire book, I honestly kept in mind the famous Voltaire quote from my high school debate team days (which may not be completely accurate in my memory, but the gist remains): "I may not agree with what you say but I will defend to the death your right to say it."

It has been more than a year since the Apollinaire issue came and went. I still wonder if those people (libraries and librarians) uncomfortable with sexually explicit materials follow Thomas Carlyle's view, that history is the study of great men and events, instead of the current social history concept that encompasses the development of humanity and its many aspects over time.[1]

Although librarians have beliefs that may conflict with their jobs, I agree with Foskett's *Creed* in his call to neutrality in which librarians are meant to shed personal identities in order to better serve patrons.[2] But the library *itself* must also shed its identity and be a neutral ground where information can be searched, requested, and found, one way or another. The library must be free of external politics. The library must be free of censorship of any kind. Sometimes I feel like I'm on a pulpit when I say such things, but I believe these things, and I'll exhort like the best tent revivalist preachers to get my point across.

Ultimately, I think it would be great to have a national library devoted to the American culture that collects everything, including the sexual bits. But until then, as I've written before in an opinion piece for *Infinity Journal*, "Academic libraries should do what they can to preserve the knowledge of our culture lest it disappears and we leave behind an incomplete record of our existence, or unfairly deny the university community access to information out of personal fears or prejudices."[3] I don't know if we will succeed in this, but I hope we do, and if so I really hope I'm around to witness it.

If I again experienced a situation like that of *Eleven Thousand Rods,* I would present the same kind argument to anyone who approached me, but I would do so knowing I wasn't alone. There has been no training on how to handle such situations at my current library or specifically in library school. The profession may put out books and provide seminars on how to handle difficult patrons, but most librarians aren't specifically told what to do if a book they've ordered gets challenged. Perhaps there is a mention that there is a form in some drawer a patron can fill out or that the irate patron can be sent to the director. The general belief among the librarians here in my library is that we work in an academic library, where all sorts of potentially offensive material can be found. We aren't here to be moral guardians or babysitters, but to provide fair and equal access. In the meantime, I continue to write opinion pieces and submit papers on this topic, being a voice among several who advocate such a collection. I would order *Eleven Thousand Rods* again even knowing about its contents, but I am less likely to order erotic fiction in general unless there is a specific literary slant or call for it.

I believe the people who were aware of this situation have come to view me in a different light, especially since I have been writing about sexually explicit topics. I take their view with good humor. There is a sociology librarian who occasionally orders books that deal with human sexuality—an example of a title recently ordered is *Manhood: The Rise and Fall of the Penis* by Mels van Driel—yet often people think I'm the one ordering the explicit books, even though they have nothing to do with my collection area, because I'm the one who ordered Guillaume Apollinaire's *Eleven Thousand Rods*. Although I do order such titles for myself, it is to add to a personal collection on my own dime. I may not be able to purchase everything, but I plan on having an extensive personal library one day.

NOTES

1. Thomas Carlyle (1795–1881) was a Scottish satirical writer, essayist, historian, and teacher. He is known for works such as *On Heroes, Hero-Worship, and the Heroic in History* (1841) in which he emphasizes "Great Men" as the motivating force of history: "For, as I take it, Universal History, the history of what man has accomplished in this world, is at bottom the History of the Great Men who have worked here."

2. D. J. Foskett, *The Creed of a Librarian: No Politics, No Religion, No Morals* (London: Library Association, 1963).

3. Michelle M. Martinez, "Learning 'about' Pornography Is Not Enough," *Infinity Journal* 1, no. 5 (2009), www.infinityjournal.com/article.php?article=100.

CHAPTER 14

Reasonable Accommodation

Why Our Library Created Voluntary Kids Cards

MATT NOJONEN

ON OCTOBER 21, 2009, a patron at our public library filed a request for reconsideration form addressing the nonfiction title *Mastering Multiple Position Sex* by Eric Garrison. The patron asked us in writing to "remove book from display case," so that children would not see it. For the sake of accuracy, it was not in a display case; it was on our new bookshelf in a face-out position. The very next day the patron visited my office. During our conversation it became clear that, literally overnight, the issue had assumed an entirely new, highly charged dimension. The book had become a symbol of what the patron described as an "appalling" decline in morals. Her point of view is best expressed in her own words, which later appeared in a local daily, the *Advocate:* "We can hardly mention the name God in our schools, but we can have this in our libraries," and "The Lord slapped me in the face with this book."[1]

No longer content to pursue relocating the item, she now wanted it removed from the collection. She also demanded that responsibility for the selection of library material be taken away from library staff and handed over to a community committee that represented "conservatives and liberals." She borrowed the book, intending to "show it to higher-ups." Before all was said and done, the "higher-ups" included our mayor, chief of police, school superintendent, a city councilman, a pastor and other church representatives, newspapers in two counties, three network affiliates in Columbus, the patron's banker, the patron's hairdresser, and a host of other citizens.

Publicity spread far and wide. Because my name had been mentioned in the article, I received e-mails from Belgium, the Netherlands, Canada,

Australia, Brazil, and all over the United States. The author of the challenged book caught wind of the situation and offered to do a free book signing. I made my first formal censorship report to the American Library Association and was surprised to learn that the Office for Intellection Freedom was already aware of the controversy. Several people were upset when they noted that in the article the patron stated her intent never to return the book. In less than a week, we received three brand-new copies from generous donors.

In no time flat, a relatively benign request to move an item from our new bookshelf to the regular nonfiction section had turned into a small-scale culture war. We had faced challenges to practically every form of media available in the library in the past, but none of them had attracted so much attention. We made it through successfully thanks to solid policies, a board that supported the policies, and a degree of carefully measured flexibility when it came to reviewing the nature and effectiveness of those policies.

THE FRAMEWORK

The library's board fully endorsed the concept of intellectual freedom in the library's mission statement and policies addressing circulation, collection development, and acceptable use of the Internet. Our collection development policy incorporates standard language, including the Library Bill of Rights, Freedom to Read Statement, Freedom to View Statement, and Ohio Children's Library Bill of Rights. These documents guided our approach and served as an excellent framework for communicating our philosophies and goals to the individuals involved and the public at large.

It's nothing new, but it deserves repeating: These policies are essential. If the policies are not in place, then there is nowhere to turn when censors come calling. The last thing any librarian or trustee should do is fly by the seat of their pants when television cameras are rolling. Above and beyond the embarrassment of appearing inept in front of the media, your community deserves a thoughtful response.

In our situation, people expressed support for the principles of intellectual freedom. They wrote, called, and made personal contact to voice their opinions. Those in favor of censorship took the time and trouble to attend board meetings and express their point of view.

Neither side of the argument would have been happy to discover that no thoughtful consideration had been given to the methods and means of providing the most fundamental service that their library offers: acquiring and loaning books. Both constituencies deserve institutional leadership that is organized and principled. Their library should operate under specific, carefully crafted, fully vetted policies and procedures.

THE RESPONSE

The patron's request to create a community committee to select library materials posed a threat potentially more damaging than the disposition of one title. Complying would have made exclusion the norm. Finding reasons to not buy an item would take precedence over diversity. Our response to the request for a community selection committee went like this:

> Collection development is not a contest of biases waged between individuals labeled "liberal" or "conservative." Censoring library selections through personal disapproval mechanisms, whether those mechanisms are "liberal" or "conservative," turns the principles of intellectual freedom upside down and replaces them with a capricious system of private opinion and private prejudice. At a practical level, the process of acquiring, processing, and making material available in a timely fashion would come to a screeching halt in a system that invited a dogmatic tug-of-war over every single item on every single order.
>
> Collection development is performed by educated, trained, and experienced individuals guided by solid legal, professional, and ethical principles. Those principles are intended to prevent individuals, including library employees, from imposing their personal, private opinions on an institution that serves a diverse community in a democratic society.

The patron's main request, that we throw the item away, was also rejected. My recommendation to the library board addressed the full range of objections that had been raised by the patron and a group of citizens who spoke at a meeting in her support. The summary determination that was communicated to the patron was as follows:

> The selection of Mr. Garrison's book is valid for the library and its users. It is protected by the First Amendment and the Constitution of the State of Ohio. The subject matter is relevant. His authority and reliability are firmly established. His viewpoint represents the diversity of ideas that our library is dedicated to preserving and providing.
>
> The determination of the Staff Selection Committee is to retain *Mastering Multiple Position Sex* in the library collection. It was also suggested that we move the title from the new non-fiction shelves to the regular non-fiction section. I concur with that recommendation. One Committee member suggested placing a cover over the jacket.

I disagree with that recommendation based on the implied disapproval that such a cover represents.

In order to reinforce the authority of parents over what library materials their children select, I also recommend that we seek guidance from the proper legal and technical authorities concerning the following draft amendment to our circulation policy.

An amendment to the library's circulation policy went through several revisions and plenty of discussion, and it was approved by our board of trustees on February 23, 2010. The amended version of our circulation policy states that "parent/s or legal guardian/s can choose to restrict their minor child's borrowing privileges to material classified by the library as juvenile."

Changing the library's circulation policy has been criticized. We completely understand the criticism. We debated several questions: Are we waffling? Are we abandoning our principles? Are we about to tumble down the proverbial slippery slope? Will some minors be unable to access important information?

I did a lot of homework before I suggested that we endorse a nuance to such a basic professional tenet. I listened to opinions on both sides, reflected on my own experience as a materials selector, library user, and parent. I reviewed previous requests for reconsideration to other library material along with the library's response to them. I reexamined applicable state statutes and pertinent ALA statements. I ran the concept past a board member who is a staunch defender of First Amendment rights.

As part of my consideration I realized that every library in my experience requires parents or legal guardians to sign a formal statement accepting responsibility for the material their minor child selects. We employ that parental authority as a defense when materials are challenged. Representatives of our profession hammer this concept home at every opportunity, in classrooms, boardrooms, and courtrooms. My conclusion was that if we adamantly and justifiably hold parents responsible, it is equally legitimate to provide them a tool that they can use to exercise that responsibility.

Allowing parents to make a decision regarding their own child's borrowing privileges does not erect an institutional barrier. The choice belongs to the parent, along with the consequences. We do not engage in case-by-case determinations at the circulation desk. If a minor whose parent/s restricted his borrowing privileges wants to take home an item from our adult collection, the parent can borrow it for him or remove the restriction from the minor's card. Eighty percent of our juvenile circulation material is checked out on adult cards, so most parents already accept responsibility for the selections of their own children, a concept that our profession insists upon.

Every child is free to access any material inside the library. No material is sequestered, and our collection development policy and mission statement remain intact. We are as free to buy Mr. Garrison's book today as we were before the amendment. We have not promised to "protect children," and according to our county prosecutor, the amendment does not creep over the line of in loco parentis. To make that as clear as possible, this disclaimer must be signed by any parent that chooses to restrict his or her minor's borrowing privileges:

> I acknowledge that the library does not contractually agree, warrant or otherwise guarantee that my child/ward will not access material from other categories besides the Juvenile collection. I agree to hold the library, library employees and the Library Board harmless from claims, losses, damages, obligations or liabilities relating to any and all use of the library's collection and services by my child or ward.

This language is almost identical to language found in most library Internet use policies. By including "services," it broadens the concept of parental responsibility to include displays, programs, and any other regular library activity or function.

The amendment to our circulation policy was not an attempt to dodge future censorship struggles or make the immediate problem go away. Patrons still have the right to challenge any item in our collection, and the decision to keep the book and leave our acquisitions process and principles unchanged had already been made. That is not to say that we were blind to community perception. It is foolish to ignore that factor at any time and particularly dangerous to do so when censorship is involved.

Establishing a voluntary means of parental control demonstrated that we were willing to entertain reasonable accommodations within acceptable bounds. Keeping the book and publicly reinforcing our commitment to First Amendment rights showed that our fundamental ethics and practices remained unchanged. The vast majority of the comments we received after the change to the library policy indicate that our community is comfortable with our decision. As of this writing, parental-approved restriction has been placed on 66 of 4,140 cards held by minors.

NOTE

1. Chad Climack, "Woman Wants Sex Book Banned from Pataskala Library," *Newark Advocate*, December 3, 2009.

PART IV

When the Tribe Has Spoken

Working with Native American Collections

We will be known forever by the tracks we leave.
—DAKOTA

WHEN a library holds information on topics related to Native American activities, history, and culture, library staff members can find themselves at a difficult crossroads. The American Library Association has developed guidelines—"Librarianship and Traditional Cultural Expressions: Nurturing Understanding and Respect"—for librarians who work with material that is sacred and important to Native American communities. Although this document offers support and guidelines, it does not and cannot address every difficult and complicated situation that comes to light in libraries holding Native American materials. The chapters in this section represent a small selection of experiences that libraries are grappling with. As the profession of librarianship continues to confront issues of access verses cultural protection, new discussions will create a better understanding of acceptable practices.

CHAPTER 15

Cultural Sensitivity or Censorship?

SUSANNE CARO

CULTURAL SENSITIVITY requires more than making sure you have copies of the Torah, Koran, Bible, Book of Mormon, Buddhist mantras, and Dianetics. It's more than having a display for Black History Month. In some cases, cultural sensitivity means sequestering materials.

I have been working with the Museum Resources Department of the New Mexico Department of Cultural Affairs to put a historic magazine online. The magazine, *El Palacio,* dates back to 1913 and contains articles on archaeological sites in New Mexico and around the world, as well as articles on Native American culture, art, and poetry. The decision was made to digitize the magazine because it is a popular historic state document and the older volumes are becoming brittle. Online access would help to preserve our paper copies while also making the content more widely available. But putting the magazine online could present some problems. The detailed information about the location of archaeological sites could place those sites at risk. We were also concerned with the photographs of native ceremonies and burials. Currently in many of New Mexico's pueblos, photography of dances, inhabitants, and buildings is not allowed. As in other cultures, many Native Americans feel that disturbing a burial is a desecration. To take photographs of human remains is also taboo. Could putting such images online be a problem?

When we asked some people within the Department of Cultural Affairs about our concerns, the first response was "you can't show that." An informal question at the Office of Archaeological Studies led to that office director's involvement and an opinion that certain information should not go online. It was implied by the people I spoke to at the Office of Archaeological Studies and others that there could be lawsuits if we put the magazine online. There was even a chance that the whole project could be scrapped by the state librarian to avoid dealing with that possibility. There was no road map for the situation—just the need for research.

Information regarding archaeological sites is protected by state law. The statute prohibits making information available that could endanger a site. When *El Palacio* was first published, archaeology was still a young field of study. The items being found were not considered to be of great value and, therefore, did not need protection. This is no longer the case, and artifacts are now worth tens of thousands of dollars. Pot hunters looking to add to their illegal collections and anyone looking for quick money might be able to use the detailed topographical maps in *El Palacio* to loot historic locations. Some of the digs described in the magazine are in areas that have been so completely excavated that there is nothing left, and others are national monuments. State and federal heritage managers are currently being contacted to determine which magazine articles might violate this law.

Next we looked at the issue of indigenous burials and ceremonies. On this issue there was no law to guide us—just good intentions. We did our research and contacted other libraries and archives with digital collections that include either photos of indigenous peoples or other possibly sensitive cultural materials such as photos of sacred items. Some institutions were willing to share their policy information; others didn't have policies. Some wondered why the question came up. Others (often archives) had been meeting with tribal advisors to help decide which materials would be digitized. One person in charge of a museum collection in another state was appalled that we would even consider the project without tribal input and was certain placing the information online would lead to a lawsuit. Tim Powell, director of Native American projects for the American Philosophical Society, was very helpful and described the process his organization uses when considering photographs to add to its digital collections. His process includes meeting with individuals from the tribes depicted in the images. The representatives of those tribes determine which photos can and cannot go online.

There is a considerable difference between individual photographs and full publications that include photographs and text. We had to think of the issues of *El Palacio* as whole objects. When dealing with photos, it is much easier to say no to a few pictures than it is to remove images and text from a published magazine. When images or text are redacted, the document is changed. What does redaction do to the integrity of the material? You are changing a historic artifact and the experience of the reader by blacking out sections. If tribal representatives wanted images or whole articles removed, would the remaining content of *El Palacio* be enough to make the project useful to anyone?

When does respect for culture cross over to censorship? We looked at several policies and best practices to try to find where the line is drawn between censorship and cultural sensitivity. The American Library Association's "Librarianship and Traditional Cultural Expressions: Nurturing Understanding and Respect" addresses the topic, and parts of it are worrisome.[1] It suggests that librarians create separate policies for user access to documents containing cultural expressions. It states that putting this information online can lead to misuse and that librarians need to "ensure appropriate use."

This seems to be at odds with the ALA's Freedom to Read Statement: "Freedom is no freedom if it is accorded only to the accepted and the inoffensive. Further, democratic societies are more safe, free, and creative when the free flow of public information is not restricted by governmental prerogative or self-censorship."[2] If a library does not buy *The Anarchist's Cookbook* because it could be misused, that is a form of censorship. If we restricted access to *El Palacio*, that would be censorship. If we removed images from the paper copies, that would also be censorship. So isn't it also censorship to remove images from the online version because of the views of one party?

Another question follows logically: If we do this for one group, will we need to do this for others? Are we willing to do this for any other segment of the population, and if not, why make any exceptions? What about Masons? They have secrets and rites that only the initiated are supposed to know, but books that expose their secret societies by author Dan Brown and titles such as *Secret Tradition in Freemasonry* stay on the shelves of libraries, as do books on Scientology that have information Scientologists object to being public. What are the requirements for a culture or group to have this kind of special status in libraries? Why make the exception for Native American cultures?

The argument for cultural sensitivity is that Native Americans have their own governments recognized by the United States, and those sovereign nations have laws regarding their cultural heritage. The United States recognizes cultural protection agreements with other countries and has a history of repatriating stolen artifacts. The Native American Graves Protection and Repatriation Act (NAGPRA) addresses objects belonging to indigenous people but does not mention images of those items.[3] Would tribal law trump state law should an issue go to court? *El Palacio* is a public document published by the State of New Mexico. As we looked for guidance on how to work with public documents, we referred to Northern Arizona University's "Protocols for Native American Archival Materials," which focuses on unpublished material.[4] Using this document as a reference, we noted that the *El Palacio* material would not be protected. We also reviewed the guidelines found in ALA's "Librarianship and Traditional Cultural Expressions" because *El Palacio* includes material described in this document as "narratives, poetry, music, art, designs, names, signs, symbols, performances, architectural forms, [and] handicrafts." The document, which was (and still is) in a draft form, suggested an unusual level of security for all library materials without considering freedom to information and public documents. The suggestion still remained: Do we redact or not when we digitize the magazine?

We were spared the hard decisions in the case of *El Palacio*. New Mexico state law prevents the custodian of state documents from altering or redacting information unless required by law. We did not have to answer these questions: Should libraries restrict access to culturally sensitive materials? Should culturally sensitive materials be locked away like some libraries treat *Playboy* or the illustrated *Kama Sutra*? Should librarians be willing to question why a patron needs a document, or how they are going to use that document? Should they "provide the necessary social and cultural context in connection with use of . . . materials in their collections"?[5] And at what point is it better to hide information and allow only certain people to view materials than to make that information available to the world? With the *El Palacio* project, articles will be evaluated to protect archaeological sites as the state law requires, but there is no law regarding culturally sensitive materials, so no redactions will be made in relation to issues of cultural sensitivity. It was also decided that the library would not develop any policies regarding digitization or cultural sensitivity.

On one hand, I love the idea of collaborating with tribal representatives to help educate the public about the vibrant and varied cultures of Native Americans past and present. I think the culture of New Mexico's native peoples should be protected. On the other hand, putting public knowledge under lock and key is not the way. It puts us as librarians on that slippery slope toward censorship.

NOTES

1. American Library Association, "Librarianship and Traditional Cultural Expressions: Nurturing Understanding and Respect," http://wo.ala.org/tce/wp-content/uploads/2010/02/tce.pdf

2. American Library Association, "The Freedom to Read Statement," www.ala.org/ala/aboutala/offices/oif/statementspols/ftrstatement/freedomreadstatement.cfm

3. National Park Service, "National NAGPRA," www.nps.gov/nagpra/

4. Northern Arizona University, "Protocols for Native American Archival Materials," www2.nau.edu/libnap-p/protocols.html#Accessibility

5. ALA, "Librarianship and Traditional Cultural Expressions."

CHAPTER 16

Developing the Public Library's Geneaology Euchee/Yuchi Collection

CATHLENE MYERS MATTIX

THE BARTLEE-CARNEGIE Sapulpa Public Library received a grant in 2008 to develop a collection for the Euchee (Yuchi) tribe based in Sapulpa, Oklahoma. We bought the very few books available pertaining to the tribe, its history, and its customs. Staff members involved in the project did a great deal of research to locate resources and gather information. We were eventually able to put together a credible collection of tribal history and social custom. We tried to work closely with tribal members in order to make this a collection that would be useful and to ensure that nothing offensive or sacred to them was inadvertently added to the collection. Through this process we discovered that books can be controversial for reasons other than the norm.

One of our staff members contacted the Columbus Museum in Columbus, Georgia, which holds a part of the tribal history. The staff member was able to obtain audiotape records from the museum, which have been digitized for the Euchee collection at our library. All participants spoke in the Yuchi language; very few people can even understand the material. The chairman of the tribe reviewed the digitized material and found nothing considered sacred by tribal custom. That fact allows the entire digitized collection of audiotapes to be added to the Euchee collection. After the material has been indexed and cataloged, it will be available for use. It should be possible to add part of this material, with translation, to our website in the future.

As we created this collection we came across *North American Sun Kings: Keepers of the Flame,* no longer in print. Its author, Joseph B. Mahan, was a scholar and professor at the University of Columbus in Georgia. In his book he presents an unorthodox view of the origin of the tribe and its arrival in the New World. His thesis conflicts with the traditional beliefs of the tribe; it is not one that they accept.

At a meeting with tribal members and the library staff involved in the project, the acquisition of the book was discussed. Library staff approached the tribe requesting input with the idea that the book be purchased if it could be found at a reasonable price. Tribal members, primarily elders, felt that the book espoused a view very different than the traditional one and therefore, many felt, the book would be an unwelcome addition to the collection. A discussion took place in which some tribal members expressed the feeling that all ideas should be available for consideration, even if they embrace a view other than that of the majority of tribal members. After the discussion, the tribal members agreed that the book could be added to the collection with a disclaimer stating that the author's views did not reflect tribal belief or custom.

The book has not yet been purchased, because of the high price of copies we have located. The staff hope to be able to add it to the collection in the near future. At that time, a disclaimer will be drafted with the assistance of tribal members.

PART V

Conversation + Confrontation + Controversy = Combustion

Vocal Organization and Publicly Debated Challenges

We are not afraid to entrust the American people with unpleasant facts, foreign ideas, alien philosophies, and competitive values. For a nation that is afraid to let its people judge the truth and falsehood in an open market is a nation that is afraid of its people.
—JOHN F. KENNEDY

AS THE American Library Association's Office of Intellectual Freedom has documented, the number of formal challenges initiated by pressure groups and religious groups accounts for a relatively small percentage of all library challenges. These organizations, however, can be extremely vocal because they often have a clear message and involve many people (sometimes national organizations). The pressure they bring to bear can come from many fronts. As the authors of these chapters explain, the challenges started by groups can rock the most stable library and trouble the most confident librarian.

CHAPTER 17

32 Pages, 26 Sentences, 603 Words, and $500,000 Later

When School Boards Have Their Way

LAUREN CHRISTOS

Local school boards may not remove books from school library shelves simply because they dislike the ideas contained in those books.

—BOARD OF EDUCATION,

Island Trees Union Free School Distric v. Pico, 457 U.S. 853

The fight for freedom in Cuba cannot be waged as a war on the First Amendment in Miami.

—ACLU STATEMENT

ON NOVEMBER 16, 2009, the U.S. Supreme Court denied a petition for certiorari from the Greater Miami chapter of the ACLU of Florida in the case challenging the removal of *Vamos a Cuba* from the Miami-Dade School District library shelves. The lower Eleventh Circuit's decision to remove the book was thus upheld. In response, the ACLU of Florida issued the following statement: "It is a sad day for free speech in our great nation. This is a dangerous precedent, and a huge leap backwards in the battle against censorship. The aftershocks may be felt in public school libraries across the country."[1]

Before we get to the conclusion of this most politically charged challenge, I would like to take you back to a particular Wednesday in late March 2006, when I first encountered what would soon become an adventure in the politics and passions of censorship, Florida style. I was at my desk in the library listening to the monthly school board meeting on the local National Public Radio station when I heard someone speaking in a fervent and passionate voice demanding that *Vamos a Cuba* be removed from his child's library. His vehemence immediately piqued my attention, and his intent came through loud and clear. Through his shouting I heard "This book must be removed!" The voice, I soon discovered, came from Juan Amador Rodriguez, a parent of a Miami elementary school student.

Rodriguez, a former political prisoner, complained that *Vamos a Cuba* avoids controversial topics, including the repressive regime of dictator Fidel Castro. He shouted, "I find the material to be untruthful" in a way that "aims to create an illusion and distort reality." Rodriguez further protested: "The book says the kids in Cuba are just like the kids here, but that is a lie! The book is correct in that in Cuba you can read, but you can only read what they tell you to. And in Cuba you can write, but be careful what you write."[2] The irony of his statement was at once startling and profound. Was he not attempting to re-create the same kind of censorship under which he was once persecuted and later fled, risking his life? As I listened to his impassioned pleas for what clearly amounted to book banning, I knew that, whatever the outcome, both Miami-Dade County and our First Amendment were in for an interesting ride. And so began a three-year legal battle in which court opinions fluctuated and over half a million dollars was spent in legal fees.

Written for students age five to seven, *Vamos a Cuba* is a thirty-two-page hardcover book published by Heinemann Library. It is a part of a small series of books in Spanish about four Latin American countries. The Spanish series fits within a larger series of children's travel books, written in English, which introduces children to twenty countries throughout the world. The full-color photographs of contemporary Cuba, its landscapes, and its people are one of the highlights of the book, which also includes bibliographical references, a glossary, a list of basic facts, and an index. Admittedly, it contains images of smiling children wearing uniforms of Cuba's Communist youth group at a carnival celebrating the 1959 Cuba revolution and states in one passage that "the people of Cuba eat, work and study like you."[3] "Nothing could be further from the truth," wrote school board member Frank Bolanos, citing food rations, proscribed employment, and forced school chants about Castro's greatness.[4] In a later memo, Bolanos stated that the book "includes content and pictures that erroneously depict life in Cuba" and continued that the book "is hurtful and insulting to both our Cuban-American community and those Cubans still living on the island under oppressive conditions."

Essentially, the complaint was that the book distorts the reality of life in Cuba. And so, on April 4, 2006, Rodriguez filed a "Citizen's Request for Reconsideration of Media." Although some of the Cuban-American community disagreed with this proposed act of censorship, the prevalent sentiment supported the removal of *Vamos a Cuba* from all Miami-Dade public schools.

I believe the first step in dealing with challenges is to understand the full issue at hand so that you can explain it to others. Knowing what outcome you would like to achieve is paramount when presenting your case to other parties. This meant that I wanted the Florida Library Association (FLA) to participate in this suit along with the ACLU and the Miami-Dade Student Government Association. This challenge clearly demanded my attention. When the case was originally filed in June 2006 (*American Civil Liberties Union of Florida, Inc., Greater Miami Chapter, et al. v. Miami-Dade County School Board*), I was chair of the Intellectual Freedom Committee (IFC) for FLA, an academic librarian at Florida International University, and a resident of Miami with two children in the Miami-Dade Public School System. I would encourage everyone to realize that participation in these civic issues is essential to a healthy democracy, and I was determined that we Floridians and librarians who believed in the First Amendment would be represented in the *Vamos a Cuba* case.

With these thoughts, I prepared a list of individuals whose support or guidance I knew I would need throughout the process. First, I posted an e-mail to the IFC electronic discussion list providing the challenge details, and I proposed that we bring the matter to the FLA board of directors. A flurry of e-mails ensued. We voted and in short order delivered our recommendation to the board that FLA join with the ACLU and lend our support. We were fortunate that there were already allies to work with, so I immediately contacted Howard Simon, executive director of the ACLU of Miami. The ACLU was committed to this challenge, and I was pleased to inform him that as a citizen, librarian, and FLA/IFC chair I was willing to do whatever I could to help. Simon asked me to find two expert witnesses who could testify for the ACLU at the court hearing. After numerous phone calls and conversations, I was able to locate two excellent librarians who were willing to testify. I also contacted my former library director, Dr. Laurence Miller, who was instrumental in sparking my interest with the intellectual freedom community as far back as 1999. I am grateful to him for his counsel. At the same time, I was working with Sol Hirsch, president of FLA, and Ruth O'Donnell, executive director of FLA, in discussing the challenge and keeping everyone apprised of our progress. And, of course, I contacted the ALA Office for Intellectual Freedom in Chicago, the ultimate source for all intellectual freedom concerns. Their outstanding staff of lawyers, advisors, and other hard working activists is a resource anyone may call upon.

The book was subsequently reviewed by the School Board Materials Review Committee with regard to suitability and age appropriateness. The review committee declined the parent's request 7–1. The committee applied the standards set forth by the school board for book acquisitions and agreed that the book should not be removed. The parent, Rodriguez, along with a politically motivated school board member, Bolanos, appealed this decision, and the issue was now brought to the district level. *Vamos a Cuba* was to be reviewed a second time, now by the District Materials Review Committee, to once again determine the suitability and age appropriateness of the book as part of the school's library collection. This committee voted 15–1 in favor of keeping both the Spanish and English versions of the challenged book. Nonetheless, the school board ignored its own committee's review process, the superintendent's decision, and the advice of its own attorney. On June 14, the Miami-Dade School Board voted 6–3 to remove the entire series from school library collections, even though the only book reviewed was *Vamos a Cuba*.

The FLA IFC began a swift e-mail discussion pursuant to this challenge. The members were extremely concerned about this act of censorship. We saw the school board's action as a clear violation of the First Amendment and recommended that FLA respond to the challenge. The timing of the ALA annual conference in New Orleans in late June 2006 was fortunate because it allowed the FLA director, FLA president-elect, and me to meet with Deborah Caldwell-Stone, deputy director of the ALA Office for Intellectual Freedom, who graciously gave us her time and counsel.

As FLA's options began to take shape and our strategy formulated, FLA's representatives became committed participants in the process of defending intellectual freedom—a core value of librarianship. Essentially, FLA could ask to file its own lawsuit as a plaintiff; it could be added to the list of other plaintiffs (ACLU and the Student Government Association) in the lawsuit; or it could file as amicus curiae. At the very least, FLA could write a resolution to the Miami-Dade School Board requesting that the books be returned to the shelves. However, at this juncture, it was necessary for the FLA board to pass a motion approving any kind of action at all. That all of this needed to happen quickly was a certainty.

After the meeting with Caldwell-Stone, I once again contacted the ACLU, which was excited that FLA was also committed. After much further discussion with Simon, O'Donnell, and Hirsch, it was determined that the best course of action would be for IFC to make a motion to the FLA board to file an amicus brief. Unfortunately, there was a strict timetable for filing. For the court to accept our brief, a July 7 deadline had to be met. This allowed less than a full week to make the motion to the

FLA board, take the vote electronically (a two-day process), and pass the motion, all before the brief was even written and filed. Acting quickly on the committee's recommendations, the FLA board voted to file an amicus curiae memorandum in the lawsuit. I was excited to tell ACLU of our progress and immediately received an e-mail from their legal director, Randall Marshall, which stated, "We deeply appreciate the interest of the FLA in this matter and believe that an amicus brief would be of immense help in this litigation."

Walter Forehand, of the law firm Lewis, Longman, & Walker, P.A., generously offered pro bono assistance, without which FLA could not have proceeded. Their generosity and expertise in representing FLA without a fee are testimony to that "network of individuals" passionate in their support of the First Amendment. On July 6, Forehand filed FLA's amicus curiae memorandum with the court. The memorandum supported the lawsuit filed by the ACLU and the Miami-Dade Student Government Association against the school board for it decision to remove the book *Vamos a Cuba* and other books in the series from school libraries. The news of FLA's filing traveled fast. The ALA's online newsletter *ALA Direct* picked up the news, as did Matthew Pinzur, the *Miami Herald* lead education writer, who covered it in his *Miami Education Blog*. The ACLU announced FLA's participation in their news.

Finally, on the overcast and rainy morning of Friday, July 21, 2006, the hearing before Judge Alan Gold began at nine o'clock sharp. Television crews and several reporters clamored outside while inside the dark-paneled courtroom preparations began in earnest to bring the merits of this case to light. For me, it was a remarkable experience to witness the process of government. Our First Amendment allows us "to petition the Government for a redress of grievances." Whatever my feelings toward censorship, free speech, and the right of free people to read freely, this was the process that our Constitution guarantees in marvelous action.

Librarian Lucia Gonzalez, associate director of Youth Services at Broward Main Public Library and member of FLA and REFORMA (the National Association to Promote Library and Information Services to Latinos and the Spanish Speaking), was one of two librarians who testified at the hearing. Librarian Pat Scales, a leading activist and defender of students' right to read for the past thirty years and author of *Teaching Banned Books: 12 Guides for Young Readers,* also testified. Their testimony was candid, direct, and forceful. The position of the school board attorneys was that the book should be withdrawn because of its "inaccuracies and omissions" regarding life in Cuba. Scales stated that, even though she had testified in numerous other hearings, she had "never testified before that a book should not be withdrawn for what it didn't say." The hearing adjourned at four in the afternoon, at which time Judge Gold stated that he would render his opinion early the following week.

The feeling after the hearing among the students, librarians, and ACLU lawyers was inspiring. I was proud to be a librarian and share in a small part of that day's experience. Three days later, on July 24 as promised, Judge Gold found in favor of the plaintiffs and issued an eighty-nine-page order stating that, "in banning the twenty-four books, the school board abused its discretion in a manner that violated the transcendent imperatives of the First Amendment," and he ordered all the books back on the shelves immediately. The books were back in the school library collections on August 14, 2006, in time for the beginning of the school year.[5]

Judge Gold's ruling was not, however, the final chapter in the *Vamos a Cuba* saga. As predicted, the school board filed an appeal with the Eleventh Circuit Court of Appeals in Atlanta. And once more the intellectual freedom community rallied. On September 22, the Freedom to Read Foundation filed an amicus brief with the Eleventh Circuit Court in the case. Joining the foundation on the brief was the American Booksellers Foundation for Free Expression, the Association of American Publishers, the National Coalition Against Censorship, the PEN American Center, the Association of Booksellers for Children, the ALA Office for Intellectual Freedom, REFORMA, and Peacefire.org.[6]

And yet, to the dismay of many, but certainly not all, the Eleventh Circuit ruled 2–1 to overturn the ruling of the federal district court judge in Miami. The court supported the Miami-Dade School Board's authority to set educational standards in Miami-Dade. The majority and dissenting opinions totaled 177 pages about a book only twenty-six sentences long.

The ACLU of Florida then appealed to the highest court of the land, the U.S. Supreme Court, to overturn the lower appellate court's decision. The Supreme Court declined to take up the case of *Vamos a Cuba*—"the little book that sparked a big controversy over alleged censorship in Miami"— thus upholding the Eleventh Circuit's decision.[7]

Kent Oliver, then president of ALA's Freedom to Read Foundation, characterized the outcome as "a very clear example of a political agenda being played out in the school library and the [district] court." Oliver went on to say that the case "really shows the importance of the First Amendment and our need to defend the right to read," explaining that the school board's removal of the book, whose cover features laughing Cuban children dressed in the uniform of the nation's Communist Party, was "about local politics trying to control the information that children access in their schools."[8] Having lived in Miami for over twenty years, I can attest to the accuracy of Oliver's statement.

At the Freedom to Read Foundation meeting I attended in 2010 at the ALA Midwinter Meeting, Foundation counsel Theresa Chmara said in her legislative update report, "While one never wants to lose a censorship case, the good part of this is that this ruling does not overturn *Pico*."[9] In fact, the concern was that, given the current Court's makeup, *Pico* could be in danger if it were to take on the Miami case. Ironic as it may be, if there is a silver lining in this chronicle, it is that by not hearing the case the Supreme Court actually upheld *Pico*.

And so, after a highly litigious three-year battle, the forty-nine copies of *Vamos a Cuba* can no longer be found on the bookshelves of Miami-Dade County schools.

NOTES

1. "U.S. Supreme Court Denies ACLU's Petition to Hear *Vamos a Cuba* Book Censorship Case," American Civil Liberties Union, November 16, 2009, www.aclu.org/free-speech/us-supreme-court-denies-aclus-petition-hear-vamos-cuba-book-censorship-case.

2. "Controversial Cuba Book Can Stay off Shelves," *Miami Herald*, November 16, 2009, Kathleen McGrory, www.miamiherald.com/2009/11/16/1337139/controversial-cuba-book-can-stay.html.

3. Alta Schreier, *Vamos a Cuba* (Chicago: Heinemann Library, 2001).

4. "Complaint for Declaratory and Injunction Relief," American Civil Liberties Union of Florida, www.aclufl.org/pdfs/vamosacubacomplaint.pdf.

5. "Order Granting Plaintiffs' Motion for Preliminary Injunction," American Civil Liberties Union of Florida, www.aclufl.org/pdfs/Legal%20PDfs/VamosOrder.pdf.

6. "Free Speech Groups Criticize Court Decision in Book Banning Case," *Book Selling This Week*, February 12, 2009, http://news.bookweb.org/news/free-speech-groups-criticize-court-decision-book-banning-case.

7. Warren Richey, "Supreme Court: Miami School Can Ban Book on Cuba," *Christian Science Monitor*, November 16, 2009, www.csmonitor.com/USA/Justice/2009/1116/p02s16-usju.html.

8. Beverly Goldberg, "Supreme Court Lets Miami-Dade's Vamos Ban Stand," editorial, *American Libraries*, November 18, 2009, www.ala.org/ala/alonline/currentnews/newsarchive/2009/november2009/vamoscaselost111809.cfm.

9. Theresa Chmara, "Legislative Update Report" (report), Freedom to Read Foundation, American Library Association Midwinter Conference, January 15, 2010.

CHAPTER 18

Respect of Fear

AMY CRUMP

In time we hate that which we often fear.
—WILLIAM SHAKESPEARE

WHEN I contemplate the actions and feelings expressed by individuals during a past book challenge at the Marshall Public Library in Marshall, Missouri, I am struck that the foundation of the intellectual freedom construct is fear. The reality is that we all experience fear and we all process it in different ways. Historically, the printed word has always had the potential to introduce new ideas, and images can increase their potency. New ideas require change. Change is scary. Words and images combined are very scary.

For some, that fear is a call to action, an examination of deep-seated beliefs and either the assimilation or rejection of the new information. The members of this group find ignoring new ideas scarier than examining them. To deny access to the information is viewed as a threat.

For others, the possibility of change is the threat. They need to know who they can consider "one of them" and who they can't. Their definition of "us" (as opposed to all those others who don't share their values, who have succumbed to evil, and so on) offers them security. To read and accept new ideas, especially ideas that have previously been taboo, requires a redefinition of their community. They fear that exposure to new information will change the entire community. They feel that protecting the community is as important as preventing censorship.

This is a story about two books that were challenged at the Marshall Public Library. I was, and still am, the library director. In September 2006, a member of the "us versus them" group submitted a request to the library board for reconsideration of two titles on the shelves of the library. One was *Blankets* by Craig Thompson, a semiautobiographical coming-of-age story. The second was *Fun Home* by Alison Bechdel, a biography that describes the author's struggle with family relationships and her own sexuality. At the time of the challenge, Thompson's book was shelved in the teen fiction area and Bechdel's was on the adult biography shelves.

The primary objection concerned the graphic format of the books, which rely on a combination of pictures and words to tell a story. Specifically, the books contain images of nudity and sexual situations. The patron felt that the format made these books attractive to young readers for whom the content was too mature.

According to the policy in place at that time, when a materials reconsideration form was received, the request was referred to the library board. The library board would hold a public hearing on the material within sixty days of the form's submission. The hearing would be advertised in the local newspaper at least one week in advance of the hearing. After the hearing, the board members would decide if the request was justified and would then take appropriate action.

Following that protocol, the hearing was held on Wednesday, October 4, 2006. Approximately 150 people attended and only a handful spoke in favor of the books. Speakers had a five-minute time limit and the hearing lasted two hours.

At the hearing, opponents of the books in question provided copies of the pages they found most offensive. One member of the audience went slightly higher tech and projected the images that were considered objectionable on the wall. The fear they felt about the images—the fear they wanted others to feel—seemed to override their common sense in displaying the images in front of the juvenile members of the audience, despite their claim that the images were inappropriate for younger readers.

Opponents of the books stated several times that the Marshall Public Library had become a source of pornography, no different than the adult stores found on the nearby interstate highway. The patron who submitted the challenge said, "The city might as well purchase the local porn shop and move it right downtown. One day, this library may be drawing the same clientele anyway." Her husband spoke to affirm that, because the library chose not to subscribe to *Playboy,* the proponents of the books could "not make this out to be a book-burning party or an attack on our First Amendment rights." Another opponent asserted, "Those who deny that the pictures are pornography merely demonstrate their mindless insistence on the absurd."

Those members of the audience who made a stand in defense of the books included a college professor who praised the books in question as "an art form." One library supporter stated, "If you only have things you like in your library, that's a private—not a public—library." Still another resident said, "No one group should be able to influence the censorship or banning of books for the entire community." In a letter sent to the board, another library patron wrote, "I choose to live free of fear and feel that knowledge gained from access to varied expressions and ideas gives me the ability to make good decisions and live wisely."

On the personal side, it was a real experience for me, being at the hearing in a room filled with people who were directing hate toward me and the board members. One woman got up and read from the Bible, turning her head to glare at me each time she read the word *Satan* out loud.

One week later, on October 11, the board held its regularly scheduled monthly meeting. The board president made a statement at the beginning of the meeting informing the audience that, in light of the absence of a materials selection policy, no decision would be made regarding the challenged books until the board had a policy in place. The policy would allow them to apply criteria to the challenged books but also to serve as a guide for materials selection for the future. The challenged books were temporarily removed from the shelves until the board had a materials selection policy to make a final decision on the materials.

A maelstrom swirled around the library and its staff during the controversy. The library's board of trustees was contacted by the National Coalition Against Censorship and mentioned on the Comic Book Legal Defense Fund website. The library received e-mails for weeks, both pro and con, and both the board and I received them as well. The local newspaper received a tidal wave of letters to the editor. In one of the letters, I was described as a dog.

In November I was contacted by David Twiddy, an Associated Press writer. He wrote an article about graphic novels in the Marshall Public Library and libraries in general. The article was picked up by newspapers around the world. At one point, I Googled the article and found it translated into at least five different languages. The book challenge was also featured in *Library Journal, American Libraries,* and *School Library Journal.* I found mention of the book challenge in three separate Wikipedia articles—on the town of Marshall, the book *Blankets,* and the book *Fun Home.* Many websites included the Marshall book challenge as part of their discussions.

The author of *Blankets,* Craig Thompson, responded to the book challenge with this:

At first I thought it was funny—how quaint. And then I thought, Wow—I thought we had progressed beyond that point in literature.

I was initially amused that a whole town hall meeting had gathered. And then I wondered, what's in [Bechdel's] book? I went and got it down off the shelf to find what they were offended by—what they would have projected on the big screen.[1]

The author of *Fun Home,* Alison Bechdel, responded that the book challenge was "a great honor" and described the incident as "part of the whole evolution of the graphic-novel form."[2]

In the December 5, 2006, issue of its statewide news journal *The Pathway,* the Missouri Baptist Convention published a front-page article that contained false information: the article stated that the Marshall Public Library had hosted the Pagan Pride Festival in 2005.[3] The publication was contacted and a correction was printed in the next edition.

While all this was going on, the library board formed a committee to create a new materials selection policy. The committee included library board members, library staff members, and me. Over the next four months we hammered out a policy primarily by examining existing library policies around the country. We presented it to the library board in February 2007. Board policy stated that a change or addition to the policy had to be proposed one month before there could be a vote on whether to adopt it or not.

In March 2007, the materials selection policy was adopted as a part of library policy by an 8–1 vote, and the board immediately applied the policy to the challenged books. Based on the policy guidelines, the two books were returned to the library shelves and made available for circulation. The only change made was that *Blankets* was moved from the young adult shelves to the adult shelves. The book, however, may be checked out by anyone who wants to read it.

The aftermath of the book challenge included at least one Sunday sermon at a local church and my name as a source of evil. The stress caused me to develop an eye spasm (which was fortunately unnoticeable in public) and a temporary paranoia that manifested itself (when I was out and about) by me evaluating everyone's faces to decide if they were friend or foe. It was painful to see how the library board members and I were portrayed and vilified—to see our life's work and dedication to integrity held up as an example of corruption and godlessness. Even two years later, a prospective employee stated that she had been told that the library director did not allow Bibles to be purchased for the library collection (which is not true, of course).

In the years since the book challenge, I understand that the fear of the unknown, or the misunderstood, is pervasive. However, just as I subscribe to the examination of new ideas and information, I support the philosophy of respecting fear, particularly the fear of others. It is not wrong to desire security or the connection of a community. To disdain those who fear change only draws out the struggle between the two groups described at the beginning of this chapter. The book challenge at the Marshall Public Library helped me gain the philosophy that to support the freedom of speech completely, you must advocate even for those who would defend something that you would dedicate a lifetime to opposing.

NOTES

1. Jennifer Pinkowski, "School Library Journal's Extra Helping," *School Library Journal,* October 2006, www.schoollibraryjournal.com/noclamp/CA6382583.html

2. Lynn Emmert, "Interviews: Alison Bechdel," *Comics Journal* 282, no. 39 (2007).

3. Brian Koonce, "Christians Strive for Clean Books in Marshall," *The Pathway,* December 5, 2006.

CHAPTER 19

Sweet Movie

SYDNE DEAN

THE PIKES Peak Library District serves a conservative Colorado community. The region is home to more than fifty religious organizations, including the very prominent Focus on the Family. The local newspaper helped to pit Focus on the Family and the library against one another in a 1992 preemptive challenge made to Madonna's book *Sex*. The adverse publicity the library endured for ordering the book (it was never received), as well as the backlash when the book was not added to the collection, was one factor in the loss of a mill levy election that year. That incident is always on our minds when we encounter a difficult challenge.

The Pikes Peak Library District does not receive an unusually high number of challenges. In 2009 we received four. Four to seven challenge or reclassification requests each year is normal for the library. But we do get "high-profile" challenges at times. In 1993, Howard Stern's book *Private Parts* came to the attention of the Colorado Springs chapter of the American Family Association (AFA). The group did not challenge the book formally, but they did alert the media, and individuals from the group wrote to me as the library's associate director. The person who led the local AFA was a self-described minister who called to talk to me and wrote to protest the book. At some point I had to call him to tell him that members of the group had written threatening letters to me personally and had labeled me a pornographer. I was not so much afraid as angry at this kind of behavior from a group professing family values. He assured me that he would stop the threats immediately, and he did. Soon after that we were invited to appear together on a radio program to discuss Stern's book.

The two of us were seated together at a table at the radio station as we waited to go on the air. We had not met in person prior to this interview.

Despite being assertive, though always polite with me in conversations on the telephone, he did not make eye contact with me when we met in person. I spoke to him first and we just chit chatted. "Nice to meet you in person." The radio host joined us and said to me, "You don't look like a pornographer." I thanked him, and we were on the air.

Any kind of media attention makes me very nervous. It is unsettling to represent the library live on the radio while discussing a difficult subject. Furthermore, Howard Stern is not someone I admire in any way. Obviously, his book had received enormous publicity, and people were interested in reading it. My argument was that patrons were free to check the book out or not, return it unread, or avoid it completely, because Stern's reputation and the contents of this book were well known. The opinions of the callers to the station probably were not changed by anything we said, but they were civil and I was grateful. The Colorado Springs chapter of the AFA is still in the area, but we have not had another incident with them.

In 2001, I was working with my third library director at the Pikes Peak Library District and had been in charge of the materials reconsideration process for more than ten years. During this director's tenure, the library had already weathered several difficult materials challenges, including against the films *The Cook, the Thief, His Wife and Her Lover; In the Realm of the Senses; Walkabout;* and *Sweet Movie.* These were all foreign films. In addition, we had handled challenges on books including *Modern Sex Magick: Secrets of Erotic Spirituality* by Donald Craig, *Mommy Laid an Egg* by Babette Cole, and *Tommy Stands Alone* by Gloria Velasquez. We were seasoned, but *Sweet Movie* was the most difficult challenge during that director's tenure with the library.

The Pikes Peak Library District purchased *Sweet Movie,* directed by Dusan Makavejev, in videocassette format in May 2001 when it was distributed by Facets in a set of six Makavejev films. The movie was initially released in 1974. The library's selector was aware of the prominent and controversial Yugoslavian director and the fact that his films had been unavailable on video since 1989. She was not familiar, however, with all of the titles in the set. The library was developing a foreign film collection at the time, but the arrival of *Sweet Movie* turned out to be anything but sweet.

The library district has a good materials review process that was put in place in 2001 and is still employed. When a patron objects to material in the library, the patron submits a form requesting the reconsideration of library material. The item is reviewed by the librarian who purchased the item and one other librarian. The associate director collects the librarians' reviews, reviews the item, and makes a recommendation to the library director. The director reviews the item and notifies the patron of the decision. A patron who is not satisfied by the decision may appeal to the board of trustees. In such cases, the trustees appoint a committee of three board members to review the item. To date, patrons have yet to request that the board reconsider an item the board has reviewed.

Sweet Movie was challenged by a patron in September 2001. The patron suggested that the movie was suitable for someone "post mortem." He called the movie pornographic, citing graphic sexual content including genitalia and pedophilia. He had watched only twenty minutes, did not search for reviews, and thought it had no artistic justification though he wrote that it had some inane symbolism. He suggested that the committee review the film and that the library put a warning label on the film or just take it off the shelves. The patron filled out the reconsideration form and gave it to a staff person working at the desk. The form was forwarded to the associate director's office. Staff members did not discuss the complaint with the patron at that time. Actually, no one ever spoke directly to this patron.

When an item is challenged, its circulation history is reviewed, professional reviews of the item are read, and staff members check to see what other libraries own the item. The reconsideration process can take a few months as library reviewers complete their reports. The time taken for reviews seems to give patrons time to decompress a little about their concerns; by the time we respond, the issue is often not so emotional. Usually, the Pikes Peak Library District, which has a popular materials collection emphasis, is mainstream in its collection, and several hundred other public libraries own an item under review. In the case of *Sweet Movie*, however, only fifteen public libraries owned the 2001 cassette. We looked to see how many libraries owned a 1989 distribution of the cassette on video tape, and there were forty holding that item, most of them academic libraries. Our library had two copies of *Sweet Movie* on cassette, and they had circulated fifty-one times from June to early September. The circulation turnover of the copies was very good—over twenty-five circulations in just a few months. The circulation record indicated that we did have a patronage that was interested in edgy foreign films. While dealing with this challenge, we removed one copy from circulation for the librarians to review, and the second copy continued to circulate.

There were many professional reviews of the movie and a lot of information about Makavejev. Adjectives used by reviewers to describe the movie included "jarring and unsettling," "taboo-busting," "audacious," "sometimes repellent," "anarchistic," "provocative," "subversive," and "not fare for normal moviegoers." Roger Ebert called the move "an experience to defy criticism . . . one of the most challenging, shocking and provocative films of recent years."[1]

Makavejev was a Belgrade native who left Yugoslavia after his film *W.R.: Mysteries of the Organism* was banned by Communist authorities. A 2001 *New York Times* article about Makavejev and the Facets release of his films states that he is "one of the boldest, most anarchic filmmakers around, an honest purveyor of cinematic treatises that explore taboo topics in the political, social, psychological and sexual arenas."[2]

The two librarians reviewed the film and their recommendations were opposite: one recommended retention, the other disposal. Both librarians were offended by the content of the movie. The librarian recommending retention cited Makavejev's body of work and the fact that the movie had been shown at the Cannes Film Festival and on the Sundance channel. The librarian recommending that the film be discarded cited full frontal nudity, no plot, sexual content, and violence. District librarians do an excellent and thorough job of reviewing items. They understand and support the ALA Library Bill of Rights, and once they make their recommendations they do not stew over the final decision.

As associate director, I reviewed the item after the two librarians. My recommendation was to retain the movie. The movie case did have a "mature audiences only" statement on it. Because *Sweet Movie* is a foreign film, there was no Motion Picture Association of America rating. The film was disturbing to watch. It would take a lot of study to figure out what the social statements were. That capitalism and communism are corrupt systems was apparent; beyond that, deciphering the images would be great for academic film study classes.

The library's director watched the movie. Normally, according to our policy, at this point he would write a letter with the decision to the patron based upon all of the information he received. He could agree with my recommendation or overturn it. But he was still very uncomfortable with *Sweet Movie*. He went outside of the policy and asked a library board member to watch the movie and weigh in. The normal process works well, and it annoyed me that we were circumventing it by going to a board member. The trustee watched the movie and stated that, although it was not a movie he would normally watch, he would not want to keep others from seeing it. We have been fortunate for many years to have board members who are strong in supporting intellectual freedom. The director was still uncomfortable with a retention decision.

We had spent a lot of time by this point discussing the movie. We talked about the ugly American theme, the obsessions attributed to capitalist Americans, and Marxism as an obvious subject of the film—illustrated by the use of a gigantic mask of Lenin on the prow of a boat. What did the river symbolize? We could not figure out much of the symbolism but, as the reviewers stated, we were not alone. The more we talked, the more I began to appreciate the movie and its untold number of nuances. One afternoon, the library director asked me to look with him at the one scene that was most disturbing to all of us—the apparent seduction of a young boy (about ten years old) by an older woman who is not fully clothed. As we watched, I told the director, "We better stop looking at this together or one of us will have to sue the other."

The scene with the boy, though disturbing, was not explicit. I would like to think that I swayed the director's thinking when I said, "Look at all of the time we have spent discussing this movie—what political statements are being made, what underlies the scenes, what was going on in Yugoslavia, etc. The fact that you can have hours of discussion about a twenty-seven-year-old movie defends retaining it."

On December 12, 2001, the director prepared the letter to the patron informing him of our decision to retain the item. In the letter he included the circulation statistics; the "mature audiences only" warning; information about the internationally recognized director, Makavejev; and the themes of Makavejev's movies, which are rooted in Yugoslavia's painful postwar experiences.

The patron accepted the decision. In the next year or so another patron challenged the movie. As a matter of policy, the library does not review items again until five years have passed from the original challenge. The second patron was sent all of the materials from the first challenge plus an updated circulation number. She also accepted the decision. And that was the last we heard of *Sweet Movie.*

Looking back, I think we were almost courageous to recommend retaining the film. Incidentally, at about the same time we were also defending Michael A. Bellesiles's *Arming America,* which was challenged by the National Rifle Association and its local chapter. Recent challenges at the Pikes Peak Library District have been routine.

Some of these challenges really test the principles of intellectual freedom. During the flap over Madonna's book *Sex,* patrons came to the library to confront me and "take my job." One patron took the opportunity during all of the coverage about Madonna to complain about the library's statue of Orpheus, which had bothered her for years. Who wants to be put through that kind of wringer again? Although some residents would come to our defense as they did with Madonna's book and with the Stern book, the majority did not and probably still would not have in 2001, and we could expect the media to keep the heat on us for some time, just as they had in 1992. Could we convince our community that this disturbing film met community standards and was tax money well spent when we also struggled with the movie? Could we stand up to media skewering of our decision? We decided that we could defend it in the public arena, if necessary.

Today the videocassette copies of *Sweet Movie* are gone—probably worn out at some point. The film is now thirty-six years old. When I searched online to prepare for this account, there were several blogs listing disturbing films. *Sweet Movie,* not surprisingly, was number eighteen on the GreenCine list of twenty-five "most disturbing movies." It is now available on DVD with new updated reviews. The Pikes Peak Library District does not own the DVD version.

As I reflect from my current perspective, I believe it was easy for me to be steadfast and black and white about reconsideration decisions. The directors, though, had the library, its staff, community support, and funding to think about, and that can be a considerable burden. Nevertheless, all five of the executive directors I have worked for have been strong in their defense of intellectual freedom, and it has been a pleasure to work with them in that arena.

NOTES

1. Roger Ebert, "Movie Reviews, Sweet Movie," *Chicago Sun Times,* January 1, 1975, http://rogerebert.suntimes.com.
2. "From Yugoslavia, a Seductive Subversive," *New York Times,* April 29, 2001, 226.

CHAPTER 20

Censorship Avoided

Student Activism in a Texas School District

ROBERT FARRELL

WHAT FOLLOWS is a story about a Christian fundamentalist group's attempt to infiltrate a large school district in Houston, Texas, by way of the school board election. One of the group's goals was to censor school libraries and textbooks. The incident took place in the 1992/93 academic year when I was a high school senior. Part of my love for libraries (I'm now an academic librarian in New York) stems from this time, when a group of teachers and students, including myself, helped avert the attempted takeover by making public the censorship planned by these candidates. Once alerted to the importance of the election by concerned teachers, students began leafleting, protesting, and attending debates that garnered citywide television news coverage. Many of those who voted to defeat the fundamentalist candidates said they would not have voted had it not been for the passion exhibited by the students in the schools. This story is about censorship avoided. The lessons are many.

School board elections were not on my mind in January 1993. Evidently, they were not on the minds of many taxpayers in the Klein Independent School District either. The public school district, located in a traditionally conservative part of northwest Houston, had an enrollment of over 25,000 students at the time and a population hovering just below 120,000. Only 5,500 voters cast ballots in the January general election, which led to a runoff between four candidates for two open seats. Of the four candidates, two were fundamentalists backed by elements of the religious right. The other two were moderate candidates whose views were more in line with the values of the larger community. Although most of the population in the area could be described as Christian and, for the most part, "churchgoing," the majority of the citizens in the area had always supported candidates who guided the district according to the leading theories of contemporary, pluralistic education—candidates who had never attempted to bring Christian dogma into the school curriculum. The Christian conservatives, who had run a quiet campaign and were supported by an active minority, had relied on the population's general contentment with the moderate status quo in order to make their initial inroad.

Once the runoff was announced, a history teacher at my high school got in touch with several students. I was the editor of the school newspaper, a known proponent of student free speech on campus, and he wondered if I'd heard about the recent school board election. Neither I nor my classmates had heard about the election. Had we, many of us would most likely have participated in the January election. I myself had just turned eighteen that December and had been actively involved in covering the previous November's U.S. presidential election for the school paper. The runoff gave us another chance to get involved, our history teacher told us. The next vote was scheduled for early February, a few weeks away. He left it at that. It was up to us to find out the details of the situation. A little bit of library research quickly filled out the picture.

What was happening in our school district had been happening across the entire country. Between the late 1980s and early 1990s, Christian fundamentalists began perfecting a strategy to win election to public school boards across the United States. Their passion was strong and their tactics shrewd. In their eyes, public education, its curricula, and its libraries introduced youth to a secular humanist perspective that undermined what they called traditional Christian values. Rather than challenge the constitutional separation between church and state, neutrally named national organizations like Citizens for Excellence in Education, Eagle Forum, and others organized local religiously active citizens to run for school board seats as a way of changing the educational system from the inside. At the time, this made a lot of sense. School board elections traditionally have a low voter turnout and don't get a lot of attention because the majority of the community is often satisfied with the way things are going. Motivate a substantial minority faction in favor of radical change, and you can swing the vote your way.

Most often, these organizations provided conservative Christians with talking points, organizational strategies, and methods for influencing the election of local officials in an attempt to create the appearance of a grassroots movement. In fact, their agenda was being advanced in a coordinated fashion across many states, particularly in states such as California and

Texas—states capable of influencing textbook design and large-scale book runs through their purchasing power. Although the religious candidates in our district's runoff did not explicitly say they hoped to censor school libraries, their use of coded language told us otherwise. As one newspaper article from the time characterized the candidates' positions, they "denied that they were for censorship, saying they did think, however, that schools could be more selective in choosing books that are proper."[1]

One of the fundamentalist candidates in the 1993 school district election had been coached and supported by Citizens for Excellence in Education and served as its local chapter president.[2] In other school districts across the country, candidates affiliated with this organization had successfully launched censorship attempts on school curricula and had legally removed books from school libraries through their control of school boards. Parent groups affiliated with Citizens for Excellence had launched successful challenges against books and curricula as well. By this point in the 1990s, the organization had become, in the words of one historian of the period, one of "the two Christian right organizations most active in trying to influence school board politics in the 1990s."[3] The founder of the group, Bob Simonds, was known for singling out specific books and authors and putting them on his followers' radar. He called one mainstream reading series a "massive occultic program" that "could cause psychological damage to the children reading it."[4] A statement he would later make in 1996 is representative of those he made at the time. Speaking of why Maya Angelou's writings should be banned, he said, "If you actually read some of her stuff, only a depraved mind would write it."[5] "We feel there is a place for censorship," he said in 1991.[6] These were not the views of our community, as evidenced by the past history of the school board. Followers of people who thought this way were not who we wanted guiding it.

The runoff election was scheduled for early February, giving us only a few weeks to act. This benefited us. The short time frame gave us a sense of urgency that helped focus our efforts. Our teachers had not given us any suggestions or advice about ways to move forward. They trusted that our own concern for free access to information would prompt us to think about ways to defend our school district, its curriculum, and its libraries. Articles in the school newspaper would not appear in time to get the word out, given our production schedule. Besides, the handful of articles about the general election and the editorial endorsement of the moderate candidates in the city's paper prior to the first vote had been ineffective. We decided that the best way to counter a sham grassroots movement was to get out and show people what a real grassroots movement was all about.

Over the next weeks, we wrote and distributed flyers expressing student concern about the future direction of the school district. We wrote that it was important to keep a diversity of opinions and materials in our curricula and libraries not only for current students but also for the intellectual growth and freedom of future students in the district. We also made it clear that local candidates taking their marching orders from outside national organizations did not represent the long-standing interests of the community. We then went to the streets, driving through neighborhoods and walking across lawns, door-to-door, to distribute the flyers in areas where voter turnout had been low.

We also knew that talking to people directly was important. We attended the two debates that were held before the runoff election and spoke out at them. We also used that time to engage parents and other voters in direct conversations about why the election was important to students. For many parents and voters, it was the first time that they'd heard young people express strong opinions about a local election. The degree of our passion for the unfettered ability of our libraries and schools to adopt the best rather than most religiously acceptable books for educating students surprised them. More important, we carried books that we knew had intellectual value but that might face challenges from Christian conservatives. I distinctly remember toting Allen Ginsberg's *Collected Poems* to various forums. Ginsberg is a writer whose work I first came across in my school library but whose subject matter, language, and sexuality would be sure to catch the eye of potential censors.

Perhaps our biggest coup was getting on our local NBC affiliate's six o'clock news. Local television still plays a major role in informing (or not informing) a population about matters of concern. At that time, during the infancy of the Internet and before the proliferation of cable news channels, its role was even more central in providing what one contemporary public intellectual has called "the social glue" of common experience within a community.[7] Knowing that the NBC affiliate would be at one of the debates, we came with our books and talking points and were soon in front of the cameras. In some sense, we were a novelty act—an articulate bunch of kids between fourteen and eighteen, fired up about a school board election. This is probably what got us the time and coverage to say our piece and get our message out to a larger group of people than we otherwise could have reached.

By the time of the election in February, we had accomplished our goal. We'd made people aware of student sentiment regarding the possibility of future censorship. The weeks between the election and the runoff were busy for everyone. Students, teacher associations, members of the local religious community, concerned citizens, and the media each weighed in on the issue. The result was an unprecedented, record-breaking turnout for the runoff.[8] Almost 11,000 voters participated, nearly double the number of the general election. The moderate candidates easily defeated the two candidates representing the interests of the religious right, nipping potential curricular and book challenges in the bud.

Other school districts at that time were not so fortunate. In the Round Rock district of Texas, a district that received a lot of publicity when religious fundamentalists came to dominate its school board, the community had been torn apart by controversies over high school reading lists.[9] As the *Austin American-Statesman* reported, quoting figures from People for the American Way, a free speech advocacy group, about one hundred candidates backed by the Citizens for Excellence in Education won election to school boards in 1993.[10] According to that advocacy group's statistics reported in *School Library Journal,* in the 1992/93 academic year there were "395 attempts to remove books and other curriculum materials from the schools," the highest number in over a decade and probably a fraction of the total attempts given the infrequency of accurate reporting. Such attempts were successful about 40 percent of the time.[11]

Among the lessons we learned, and one I still carry with me today, is that young people can be a major force in motivating voter turnout and generating excitement in situations where they may not be considered serious stakeholders. How much impact did our student movement have in the end? It's hard to say. In a follow-up news broadcast, several local voters were interviewed about the election and stated that they probably wouldn't have made the effort to vote had it not been for the student activism. That we cared so much about the issue got them to care. We heard the same thing anecdotally from parents and teachers.

Important to our effectiveness was our independence. Although our teachers alerted us to the existence of the situation surrounding the election and impending runoff, they did not interpret it for us or tell us to do anything. We mobilized ourselves and developed our own strategy. We wrote our own material and distributed it ourselves. We thought for ourselves and expressed ourselves, sometime boldly, sometimes nervously, but always authentically. Anyone looking to get young people involved in censorship issues should be aware that there could be the appearance of adult manipulation. Trust kids to inform themselves and make intelligent decisions.

Small elections can have enormous impacts. This is another lesson we came away with. School boards were not the only public bodies targeted by the Christian conservative movement at that time. Hospital boards and other forms of local government faced, and still face, these same challenges.

Small-scale democratic institutions create the everyday forces that shape peoples' lives, give people opportunities, or cut such possibilities off. Censorship is worrisome, but perhaps more worrisome are the consequences of unseen censorship in school districts dominated by small-mindedness or ideological bias: the crippled curricula, the books that never reach the shelves of libraries. This form of censorship can go on in a hidden manner for years without anyone becoming aware of it.

Last, we realized that it's much better to fight today against the possibility of censorship than to fight tomorrow against a censoring school board or an entrenched local extremist group. By stopping the representatives of the religious right from gaining board seats, we were able to preclude potentially covert censorship from above. Through the publicity resulting from the election battle, we also alerted community members to the growing threat of religious extremism in this seemingly innocuous area of civic life. As a community, we sent a message to national religious organizations that our district was not up for grabs, thereby precluding potentially overt censorship from below.

Citizens for Excellence in Education and its parent organization still exist. Rather than simply distributing audiotapes and pamphlets to followers, its founder now presides over a website. He's always had a radio show. He says that he's now encouraging members of the religious right to abandon the public schools altogether, but he still sells his book *How to Elect Christians to Public Office*. Local communities have awakened to the possibility of "stealth candidates" from the religious right since the 1990s, but voter apathy or distraction is always with us. Teachers and librarians can keep talking about censorship past and censorship present, censorship actual and censorship avoided, in order to engage students and the community in ways that keep everyone vigilant. There will always be special interests of one sort or another. Unlike dogmatists who seek to silence the voices with which they disagree, defenders of free information seek to know, not censor, the views of those very dogmatists in order to keep pluralistic ideals strong and the ideas of those who would oppose them in the open, where they can be seen for what they are.

NOTES

1. Melanie Markley and Ruth Piller, "Christian Fundamentalists Lose Klein School Board Runoffs: Heated Contests Result in Record Turnout of Nearly 11,000," *Houston Chronicle*, February 7, 1993, A13.

2. Stefanie Asin, "Group Aims for Pro-Religion School Boards," *Houston Chronicle*, January 26, 1992, C1.

3. Melissa M. Deckman, *School Board Battles: The Christian Right in Local Politics* (Washington, D.C.: Georgetown University Press, 2004), 172.

4. Kevin Diaz, "Parental Challenges to 'Satanic' School Books on Rise in State," *Star Tribune* (Minneapolis, Minn.), September 21, 1992, 1A.

5. Gloria Goodale, "Who Decides Which Books a Child May Read?" *Christian Science Monitor,* December 6, 1996, Books 11.

6. Nanette Asimov, "State Said to Be a Prime Target of Censor Groups: Yearly Report on Book Bans in US Schools," *San Francisco Chronicle,* August 28, 1991, A13.

7. Cass R. Sunstein, Republic.com 2.0 (Princeton, N.J.: Princeton University Press, 2007), 97.

8. Markley and Piller, "Christian Fundamentalists."

9. Cindy Rugeley, "Religion, Sex Education Keep Texas Schools in Turmoil," *Houston Chronicle,* January 2, 1994, A1.

10. A. Phillips Brooks, "Movement Targets School Boards with 'Moral Direction,'" *Austin American-Statesman,* March 6, 1994.

11. M.J.S., "41% of Censorship Attempts Successful, New Report Says," *School Library Journal* 39, no. 10 (1993), 10.

CHAPTER 21

I Read It in the Paper

HOLLIS HELMECI

THIS EXPERIENCE of censorship is somewhat unusual in that, although I was the director of the public library in question, I knew nothing about a complaint against a book in our collection until it was published in the newspaper. The first formal complaint was made during a city commission meeting, and the coverage in the local newspaper was my source of information. I have reconstructed the time line for this incident on the basis of publicly available information and from conversations with the library staff. At the time of the complaint, the materials in question were being processed in library offices and were therefore not available to the public.

The complaint involved a set of graphic novels, Blazin' Barrels, which were purchased from a reputable company (Delaney) that serves schools and public libraries. The books this company offers are relatively well screened to be appropriate for school-age patrons and were purchased by our library to invigorate and expand the young adult collection. The series was selected specifically for the young adult area of the collection, which is on a separate floor from the children's department.

The complaint focused on graphic novels in general and on the cover of Volume 3 of the Blazin' Barrels series in particular. One individual indicated that she believed they belonged in the young adult area, not in the children's area (her understanding was that the children's area was the intended area for this series). If the woman had discussed this with me, she could have been assured that the materials were going to be placed in the young adult area, not the children's area. A second person, who complained to the city commission directly, claimed that the cover showed a bare-breasted woman and contained dirty words in large print. She implied that the library was putting pornographic material in the children's collection (a collection that is intended for infants through fifth grade).

At that time, all young adult materials were cataloged by the children's department, so the items were kept in the cataloging/processing area for the staff to access them easily. The materials were visible to the public, but to see any particular item, one had to enter the staff work area. In other words, to see the cover of a book, a patron would have to be shown it by a staff member or would have to walk into the work area and take the material off the shelf.

The mayor and the commissioners expressed an interest in discussing this with the library director, but I never heard from any of them about this issue. A day or two after the commission meeting, I did have a board member ask me about these books. It was during my discussion with the board member that I determined that the books were still in processing, for we could not find them on the shelves. At this point in the scenario, I realized that a staff member must have shown the material to the patrons, or that the patrons must have freely entered the staff work area.

I had three staff members look for the "dirty words." No one found offensive language in "large letters." This may be due to a difference in standards for "dirty," but it seems likely that if the words were in "large letters" they would be easily found. Because the complaint did not provide the actual words under discussion, it was doubly difficult to locate the "offensive" words. The staff members did find that one character on the cover had a revealing dress and determined that it was either improbable or impossible to wear that dress given the physical activity depicted, but no one on the staff thought the cover was obscene or inappropriate for young adults.

The specific cover has two young women running, carrying guns, and one has considerable cleavage showing. Near the bottom of the cover another character, apparently male, is visible. The woman with the "bare" cleavage is built like Barbie, but her breasts are not bare—significantly, her nipples are not visible. The other young woman is fully covered.

I brought the matter to the attention of the board at the next meeting and shared with them a photocopy of the cover, as well as the fact that three of us had looked for the "dirty words" but could not find them. I explained to the board that the graphic novel series had always been intended for placement in the young adult section, and that no one had come to me to discuss these concerns.

There were no written complaints filed at the library, as required by board policy. The board felt that this was a matter they could dismiss without further discussion because the library policy had not been followed. The board members were unsettled by the two challengers' behavior and very public complaints; this issue was creating a great deal of negative newspaper coverage for the library.

The situation received so much press because an employee had just been fired, and the books' two challengers were very supportive of that individual during the city commission meeting. In other words, in their highly vocal support of the employee, these women apparently were using their complaints about the library's books as a way to legitimatize their attacks on the library and library director. When the matter had settled, mostly of its own accord, one of the women did say she would not be using the library again because she did not care for the way it was run. But even following this confrontation, there was never a formal complaint filed about the books in question.

This incident was unsettling in that there was never any real resolution, just as there was no official complaint. As a learning experience it certainly allowed me, as the director, to develop steps for handling major issues internally. The lack of interest or follow-through from the commissioners was both a blessing and a disappointment, because I was not required to discuss the matter with them, but I also lost an opportunity to forge any kind of relationship with them and tell them about the library's public interactions. Because I had been at the library a very short time and had never encountered this kind of situation before, I was hesitant to contact commissioners who were clearly not actively seeking to speak to me. Perhaps I would be more active in seeking information and opinions should any such situation occur again.

Because the library board members were never contacted about these books, it put this incident into a peculiar status. It was almost as if no one was responsible for answering this highly public yet unofficial complaint. The board chose to maintain a studied distance from this matter, and I followed their example. Given the way the patrons handled this matter, it allowed everyone associated with the library to maintain a "hands-off" response, which may have been the best way to deal with this situation.

The furor died, and the board felt that the materials were acceptable for the intended patrons. There have been no complaints from parents about the content of the graphic novels, and the library has continued to add other graphic novels to the young adult area.

In the time since the challenge occurred, the library has begun to actively use the rating system that is printed on some books (13+, etc.) if they are in the area for any young adult to read. The library staff explain that this system is just like a movie rating system, which seems to satisfy most people. Because some graphic novels have an age-appropriate rating printed on the book, the library has used these as a guideline, just as with movies. There are parents who do rely on the publishers coding to determine if they want to allow their children to read these novels. The library also uses the coding as a guideline so that staff are aware of material that may not be fully appropriate for younger patrons. The use of these publisher-created ratings is intended not as a step to deny younger readers access but to ensure that everyone using these materials is aware of the intended audience's age. All the ratings on the graphic novels are taken directly from the books themselves.

There have been requests for specific graphic novel series by patrons that indicate the interest in this format. As with all requests, they are considered and may or may not be filled depending on the budget and a judgment about whether the items have a broad enough appeal. There are also occasional comments from patrons about the common sense of people who read graphic novels, but no official complaints.

The fact that the board felt free to dismiss the complaints about the Blazin' Barrels series because the challengers did not follow the required process is a strong argument for having a written policy that delineates the steps necessary to challenge library material. Having a written form, which the board expects patrons to use, provides a clear demarcation for everyone in a situation such as this. When a complaint is used as part of another agenda, which does happen, having a process in place is both vital and sensible.

CHAPTER 22

Uncle Bobby's Wedding

JAMES LA RUE

THE DOUGLAS County (Colorado) Libraries has received many written challenges to library materials—more than two hundred in the twenty years I have been its director. There are several reasons for this. Foremost among them has been demographics. Douglas County, from 1990 to 2000, was the fastest-growing county in the United States. Most of the newcomers were baby boomers raising their own kids. As I noted in my book *The New Inquisition,* there is a generational dynamic of rising protectiveness—even overprotectiveness—of children.[1] Many of today's parents, especially parents of children leaving infancy or on the cusp of young adulthood, simply don't want their children to know how difficult or complex the world can be. Parents want to preserve their children's innocence or, at least, the illusion of innocence. This desire is motivated by both love and grief. Yet children's literature is a powerful way for young ones to make sense of the world, to prepare themselves to survive and thrive.

Another factor has been geographic. Douglas County is just north of Colorado Springs, headquarters of Focus on the Family. In the early 1990s, this radio ministry identified "the gay agenda" as a matter of particular worry, as well as the alleged family-unfriendliness of the public library. Focus on the Family's publications and broadcasts pressed the issue frequently. The tone of outrage, of beleaguered parenthood, of angry righteousness helped provoke many heated encounters between parents and librarians in Colorado.

Yet another factor was administrative. In accordance with library policies, I personally responded to each written challenge. Unwittingly, I think I established a culture in which staff responded to even the mildest verbal complaint by giving the patron a request for reconsideration form. The form encouraged written challenges and discouraged more thoughtful dialogue. These days I encourage my staff to listen first, then seek to resolve the issue with good service, finding something patrons do want rather than focusing on what they don't. Now the form is the last, not the first, step. Only a supervisor can distribute one. I think our patrons are better served. In the past year, the number of our formal challenges has dropped significantly, and use of our collection has risen.

GAY CHALLENGES

The many challenges over the years have tended to fall into a few perennial categories. One was fairy tales; another, sex education. But by far the most challenged specific titles were *Daddy's Roommate* and *Daddy's Wedding,* both by Michael Willhoite. Both books positively portray an adult gay relationship from the perspective of the son of one of the men.

I responded in writing to the many challenges about these items; I always chose to retain the titles. Indeed, I pointed out that I first bought the books as a direct result of a patron request. A woman told me that her husband had left her for another man, and she was trying to find a way to talk about the situation with her preschool-age son. She found *Daddy's Roommate* helpful.

Another challenge was to *Alfie's Home* by Richard Cohen. This book presented the notion that homosexuality is a psychological confusion that can be cured through counseling and Christian faith. As a book, I found it far less convincing than Willhoite's work. *Alfie's Home* is preachy and faintly alarming (the young protagonist's interest in same-gender sex seems to be the result of a distant and abusive father and a sexually exploitative uncle). But by buying it, we demonstrated our willingness to portray at least two sides to the issue. I kept that title too, although it was eventually removed due to lack of use. We replaced it with Cohen's *Gay Children, Straight Parents: A Plan for Family Healing.*

Incidentally, Willhoite's books eventually didn't get used much either and have also been weeded. Likewise, other titles have replaced them, including Sarah Brannen's *Uncle Bobby's Wedding.* This is an important point. Materials from both perspectives are treated the same: they are acquired when they're new, but in the modern library, books from any viewpoint have to earn their place on the shelf. Either they find readers, or they make way for newer materials.

ELECTIONS AND FORMAL CHALLENGES

In the early summer of 2007, my library board decided to go forward with a campaign for a mill levy increase. Douglas County is overwhelmingly

Republican. The library did very well in various polls: we had an approval rating of over 94 percent, some 84 percent of our households had at least one active library card, our annual average circulation per capita hovers around twenty-seven, and over half of our surveyed voters indicated support for our modest increase (which would have gone mostly to capital construction). But there is also a strong anti tax sentiment often expressed by party officials, politicians, and letters to the editor.

As it happened, we lost the election. It was heartbreakingly close: 210 votes, just barely 1 percent of the total count. It was close everywhere; we lost mainly because of the votes of one town that had a new and fairly large library. But the need for the rest of the county remained, and we decided to launch one more campaign, counting on the higher turnout of the 2008 election to see us through.

So it was in this context that on June 26, 2008, a woman wrote two letters protesting the library's ownership of *Uncle Bobby's Wedding*. One letter was published in the local newspaper; the second letter came addressed to me at the library. The former was more pugnacious; it called for citizens to rise up in their outrage. The latter was more diplomatic; it urged cooperation and accommodation. Specifically, it recommended the placement of the book in a special "parents only" section of the library.

Uncle Bobby's Wedding tells the tale of a group of very well-dressed and caring guinea pigs, and in particular of young Chloe. Chloe is worried that her favorite uncle, Bobby, won't have any time for her after his impending marriage. The marriage is to another male guinea pig. Eventually, though, it all works out; Chloe learns to like Uncle Bobby's partner and even winds up being the flower girl for the ceremony. The narrative voice and illustrations are altogether charming.

The points of the complaint were these: the topic of gay marriage was itself inappropriate for the age group of a children's collection; gay marriage was contrary to the definition of marriage in the dictionary, contrary to the spirit of our nation's founders, and contrary to the Bible; and the purpose of the book was to promote the idea that gay marriage was acceptable.

In addition to launching this two-pronged attack (public and private letters), the written library challenge was unusual in two other respects: it asked for a response to be e-mailed rather than written, and it pointed out that the letter's author had many friends who felt the same way she did (although she also indicated on the request for reconsideration form that she was not representing anyone but herself).

It did occur to me at the time that the challenges might have an overt political aim: the defeat of our mill levy proposal.

I responded to the letter to the editor on the editorial page, coincidentally the day before Independence Day. I took the opportunity to write about the background of the First Amendment. Our freedom from censorship was nothing if not American, the very driving force of our founders: the right to speak one's mind and conscience, to be free of government restraint in such matters, and in particular from the intersection of religious and political orthodoxy, or "the tyranny of the majority."

At the same time, I wrote and e-mailed a particularly detailed response to the challenge, believing that it would be widely distributed to potential political opponents, so taking care to set a tone of reasoned respect. Later I decided to preempt its distribution by posting it on my blog, which I did on July 14, 2008.[2]

I informed the patron that I had decided to retain the title, but in accordance with our policies (which I attached to the blog post) she could appeal that decision to the library board.

I received two more challenges within a week or so: one almost a copy of the first, and another asking if I preferred to get the challenges one at a time or in the form of a petition. I responded in writing to both of them, again deciding to retain the titles and offering to meet with whatever group had such concerns to discuss the issues freely.

That strategy was deliberate. A frequent tactic of those who challenge library materials is to allege that librarians themselves do not practice free speech, by which they mean open discussion of the issues. I was determined to demonstrate the falseness of that.

As far as the challenge was concerned, that was it. I never got another letter or phone call. I was not invited to meet with any group. On the other hand, there were several more letters to the editor on both sides of the issue, with most of them trending in favor of firm opposition to censorship. One letter strongly suggested that the county would be better off without me and that, of course, the library lost elections with such liberal attitudes in place at the top. Soon after this, that letter's author was chosen as the leader of the local Republican Party.

I should also note that we did in fact lose the second election, this time by some 7,000 votes, although the recession may have had something to do with it. The central committee of the local Republican Party believes they killed it, and that the "gay issue" helped activate their base.

LIFE IN THE BLOGOSPHERE

The responses to the blog posting came in waves. The first was triggered by the author of the book, and by me. I later interviewed Sarah Brannen and she told me that she had set up a Google alert about her new book.

My blog posting was one of the first to come through to her as an alert and marked the first report of a challenge to it. She passed along the link to her publisher, editor, and friends. Thenceforth, it spread to the LGBT community. In turn, I had passed along the posting to various librarian friends who put it in their blogs and newsletters.

The second wave resulted from being picked up by the larger blogo-sphere. Most of the commenters reported where they had heard about it: LiveJournal, Digg, Bitch Ph.D., mental_floss, Reddit, kottke.org, and Twitter.

I had turned on site visit tracking back in May, when I was getting about two hundred visits a month to my blog, with a little over four hundred page views. (A visitor is a "session" of use, so likely an individual reader; "page view" includes views of a page or pages during that session.)

In July, when I first posted this thread, visits jumped to 26,472, with 32,334 page views. On July 31, 2008, there were 12,183 visits on one day.

In August visits jumped to 26,987, with page views up to 34,710.

By October the blog was back down to about 300 to 600 visits a day. People were coming to that one thread 80 percent of the time .

The third wave came almost a year later in September 2009. The traf-fic can be attributed to two postings: a link at the bottom of the popular A.Word.A.Day, and a tweet by author Neil Gaiman. That September I got 35,000 page views, and in October, 57,000. Since then my blog page views hover around 2,000 a month.

At this writing there are 434 comments.

THEMES

It's the comments that interest me. Commenter Dan said, "I am intrigued by the shift in the central focus of controversy that seems to have occurred during the month of August [2008]—a shift away from the patron's com-plaint or the content of the children's book in question and toward the status and purpose of the library system." That was an astute observation. There were several themes in the comments.

The Gay Divide

One theme is what I'll call "the gay divide." At this moment in our cul-ture, any book about homosexuality, particularly around the presentation of that topic to children, is a flash point. The comments here fell across the spectrum. On one side were the handful of folks who asserted, usu-ally on the basis of their Christianity, that *Uncle Bobby's Wedding* was gay propaganda targeted at children and must be stopped. The general tenor of these remarks tended to be harshly judgmental and absolutist. At the other end were people who dismissed—with considerable anger, vulgarity, and name-calling—the first group.

As I noted in my own comments, a sign of our times is the demand that propaganda cease—unless it's your own.

But in the vast middle were others with far more interesting perspectives. Some said they were Christian and had real reservations about something their religion pretty clearly, they thought, condemned. Yet they recognized that not everyone shared their views. They asserted only their right to teach their own children their values. Others reported that they either were or were not Christian or gay but didn't see what the fuss was about. They liked knowing that a gentle book encouraged greater acceptance and tolerance of others.

To my mind the most touching stories were from gay people themselves, many of whom reported trying to find books in the libraries of their youth about people like themselves—and in the absence of such books concluding that they must indeed be outcasts. The silence of our libraries on the topic, to my mind, had damaged lives.

Clearly, at this moment in our national consciousness, we have not reached consensus about the level of acceptance of gay people into our society, but I am heartened to report strong evidence of compassion.

Cry for Civil Discourse

A second theme of the responses was about the fervent desire among many for thoughtful and respectful civic dialogue. This was expressed sometimes in direct and complimentary language, and sometimes as humor. Many remarked that such civil civic dialogue is both rare and welcome. And so it is. We live instead in a time of foaming rhetoric and snarkiness. But short of persuading people that those who are loudest are the majority (a statement I would dispute), such rudeness really doesn't change anyone's mind; it just seeks to bully them into shutting up.

The Role of the Library

A third theme focused on the mission of the public library. Looking over my responses, I notice that I tended to respond more to the fierce critics than to the folks who had kind words. I should think more about that; that means that the critics get more attention. Such a strategy probably grows critics.

But the challenges to my letter, when they were not so much about the content, were about the imputed purpose of the public library, a belief that it had only one job—to warehouse books, and apparently books that reflected only a majority bias. There persists in our culture a general feeling that libraries are good things, but also that they belong in the background. To my mind, it is hard to both promote literacy passionately and be invisible.

One of my statements in the blog posting has been widely quoted: "Library collections don't imply endorsement; they imply access to the many different ideas of our culture, which is precisely our purpose in public life." I believe that it's important for us to underscore that purpose.

WHAT DOES IT ALL MEAN?
The publication of this letter, which addressed the concerns of the patron respectfully but spoke without apology to the value and purpose of the public library, accomplished several positive things:

It upheld our own policies in defense of intellectual freedom.

It provided, at least in some respects, a model for civic engagement in which the goal is conversation, not confrontation.

It provided a public forum, not only for consideration of a hot topic of our culture, but for a deeper examination of the role of the library. Clearly, that role—as both common and neutral ground, as a proud and confident explorer of our culture—has yet to be fully embraced by our citizens, or our netizens.

We can't allow others to define us into irrelevance or silence, but the only way to withstand that trend is to engage with the larger culture. We must add our voices to the intellectual environment in which we operate, advocating our vital role. Blogs, wikis, and social networking all offer us powerful new tools to do just that.

NOTES
1. James LaRue, *The New Inquisition: Understanding and Managing Intellectual Freedom Challenges* (Westport, Conn.: Libraries Unlimited, 2007).
2. James LaRue, "Uncle Bobby's Wedding," *Myliblog*, entry posted July 14, 2008, http://jaslarue.blogspot.com/2008/07/uncle-bobbys-wedding.html.

CHAPTER 23

A Community Divided

KRISTIN PEKOLL

WHAT MADE our challenge unique is that it didn't start with a book. Our challengers (a whole family) were upset with a list. In their original letter—deposited in our book drop—they claimed that during a recent Google search for the library they were directed to a young adult website titled *Out of the Closet: Gay, Lesbian, Bisexual, and Transgender Fiction and Non-Fiction.* They provided examples of sentences they found offensive and closed with

> As a conservative community, I am sure the taxpayers of West Bend [Wisconsin] would be as offended as my husband and I were when we reviewed this website that directly links itself to our very own West Bend Community Memorial Library. Therefore, I am bringing this to your attention and ask for an explanation as to who is responsible and accountable for its creation, and asking that it be removed at once.

Our library director and I (the young adult librarian) were unsure how to handle the letter because we had never encountered a complaint about the library's website, and our reconsideration policy wasn't designed to cover online resources. The confusion over how to deal with the website was resolved two weeks later when we received a formal reconsideration form from the same family listing thirty-seven book titles for library reconsideration.

So much happened the first month the letter appeared. The library was on the front page of the newspaper, headlined "Gay Link." There were daily letters to the editor criticizing our judgment and our unwillingness to help families protect children. Voice mails and e-mails directed to us personally attacked our morality and common sense. The challengers had a family blog that didn't refrain from sharing their opinion of the library and the librarians.

People would come to the desk and ask for "those books," referring to the thirty-seven challenged books. Along with the original thirty-seven titles listed in their formal reconsideration form, the family included all the books listed in the *Out of the Closet* book list as well as many more, well over eighty books total. They were labeled "gay propaganda," "sexually explicit," and "child pornography." The four books receiving the most attention were *Geography Club* by Brent Hartinger, *Deal with It* by Esther Drill, *The Perks of Being a Wallflower* by Stephen Chbosky, and *It's Perfectly Normal* by Robie Harris.

During the next few months, other organizations got involved, on both sides of the issue. Among these were Safelibraries.org, University of Wisconsin–Milwaukee, American Civil Liberties Union of Wisconsin, Cooperative Children's Book Center at University of Wisconsin–Madison, Wisconsin Library Association, American Library Association's Office for Intellectual Freedom, Gay Lesbian Straight Education Network, Parents and Friends of Ex-Gays, and Parents Against Bad Books in Schools. Many spoke out publicly, wrote letters, and came to the library in support. Angela Maycock and Deborah Caldwell-Stone from ALA's Office for Intellectual Freedom came up from Chicago during our community-organized read-in to talk about censorship. Deborah Caldwell-Stone spoke at our library board meeting about the illegalities of censoring books and moving books to other collections.

The community was divided into two groups: those who agreed with the very vocal West Bend Citizens for Safe Libraries, and those who agreed with the newly formed West Bend Parents for Free Speech. There were petition signings, protests on street corners, marches, read-ins, and a float in the Fourth of July parade with a washing machine declaring the library "unclean."

A local alderman who never set foot in the library verbalized opinions at a city council meeting that were later quoted in the newspaper; he called the library a "porn shop." When a library board member told him that the library was following policy, he replied, "I don't care what your policies are, I want those books off the shelf." That same library board member and three others were denied reappointment by the city council. Our small West Bend town made national news when a group of four men from Milwaukee, calling themselves the Christian Civil Liberties Union, sued the library for emotional damages to the tune of $120,000 and demanded that the book *Baby Be-Bop* be publicly burned in front of the library. As far as the library is concerned, the lawsuit and book burning faded away. The lawsuit was directed to the city attorney and insurance, and we have not heard from the Christian Civil Liberties Union since.

The library board decided to hold a special informational meeting to discuss young adult materials and their location in relation to the children's department and the adult department; any community member could speak for two minutes to address the board and voice an opinion. After three hours, the library board shared its thoughts and voted unanimously to maintain the young adult collection without removing, moving, labeling, or restricting any books in any way.

Although the decision has been made, our community is still divided. I often wonder how much of what has happened in the past year is a play for power in the community. Citizens often respond with "I know my community!" and "I want to protect the minds of our children." When the challengers first brought forth their complaint, they didn't want to speak to me or the director; they wanted to go right to the top, to the library board. And when the board didn't respond as they wanted, they went to the mayor and the city council. When the city council couldn't change the decision of the library board, they voted for new people to serve on the library board. It seems that there was a constant one-upmanship of power. Even now, a year after the library board decision was made and the library board has been completely overhauled, there's talk of getting rid of the mayor.

In some ways, I'm glad this has happened. It is great to see parents involved in what their kids are reading. People are taking an interest in how their local government works and are being active in the process. It is the truest form of democracy to watch people voice their opinions to their elected officials. We have to protect that right just as closely as we protect the right to read and to have access to all forms of knowledge. It has also brought a national spotlight to the issue of censorship and how important it is to fight against it in all of its forms: labeling, recataloging, permission slips, and hiding books.

Last year when I decided to stand up for over eighty books in the West Bend Community Memorial Library's young adult collection, it wasn't because I thought every single book on the list was gold-star material. It was because I believe that every book has a reader and every reader has a book. When you deny that person, especially that teenager, his or her book—when you ban that book—you ban that kid.

CHAPTER 24

The Author Visit That Should Have Been

KARIN PERRY

AS A middle school librarian, it is important for me to provide a variety of books, both in content and reading level, for the students in my building. This can be a challenge because my students range in age from eleven to fourteen, but in my nine years of school librarianship every student seemed to have found something they liked to read. Sixth-grade boys enjoyed the Shredderman series by Wendelin Van Draanen, and eighth-grade girls devoured The House of Night and Vampire Academy series.

All kids are different. They have different experiences, different emotional needs, different tastes; the list goes on and on. One eighth-grade boy may love reading *Epic* by Conor Kostick or *Ender's Game* by Orson Scott Card; another may find those unique science fiction novels too complex and prefer to read *Aliens Ate My Homework* by Bruce Coville. Not every eighth-grader is developmentally ready for a book like *Crank* by Ellen Hopkins, and the flip side is also true: some sixth-graders are able to handle the intensity of a book like *Go Ask Alice*.

As a school library media specialist, I always tried to stay up-to-date on the books being challenged around the United States. I felt sympathy for the teachers and librarians in the middle of such controversies and was thankful to be living in a community that rarely jumped into hysterics over the contents of a book. In the eleven years I worked in my school district, I was aware of only one incident that resulted in the use of the reconsideration policy the district had in place.

The reconsideration policy provides the guidelines the district must follow to remove a book from the library or classroom. It specifies who is placed on the reconsideration committee, the committee members' responsibilities, and which members can and cannot vote on whether or not a book should remain in the school. I always knew that having a reconsideration policy was important, but never was I more aware of the need for one than in our 2009/10 school year.

That year was my ninth as a school library media specialist. I had spent four years in an elementary school and was now working in a middle school setting. Middle school seemed to be the perfect fit for me. Not only was I surrounded by quirky, hormonally crazed kids, but I also got to spend my time reading the type of literature those students were drawn to—young adult literature. When the thought of challenged books came to mind, I considered myself lucky for never having had a book from my school's collection come under fire—that is, until September 2009. What started out as a major coup on my part turned out to be the most challenging experience of my library career.

My censorship story began in May 2009 when I was lucky enough to win an author visit for my school from best-selling author Ellen Hopkins. I was able to secure her visit for about one-fifth of her regular speaking fee. I was absolutely thrilled that I would be able to bring such a popular and well-known author to my school for the eighth-grade students. Because May was too late in the year for an author visit, Mrs. Hopkins was kind enough to put off the event until the next school year. After the scheduling was complete, I notified my principal (a past middle school language arts teacher) and my district library director. Everyone was excited.

The beginning of the school year is always busy, but when this year started the eighth-grade language arts teachers were willing to open up their classrooms to allow me to prepare the students for Ellen Hopkins. When I visited their classrooms I shared short booktalks on each of Hopkins's books, exposed the students to her poetry style, showed Hopkins's website, and offered students the chance to purchase books for autographing. I purchased copies of *Crank, Glass,* and *Impulse* for the students to buy. I sent home an order form with the prices, and by the Monday before the author visit the books were sold out.

On Tuesday, September 15, the day after I ran out of books, a parent lodged a complaint with my principal about *Glass* and the author visit. She wanted the book removed from the library, and she wanted the author visit canceled. My principal informed the parent that, if she wanted the book removed, she was welcome to fill out the district's reconsideration form. The principal went on to tell the parent she had every right to remove her child from the room while the author spoke, but that Ellen Hopkins would still speak at the school the following week. The principal came to my office as soon as the parent left to fill me in on the details of the confrontation. I was disappointed and a little nervous, but for the most part I felt confident. My principal had supported me, and I thought that as long as the parent followed the procedures laid out in the policy everything would be okay.

My feeling of confidence didn't last long. Within a couple of hours my principal paid me another visit, this time to tell me the parent had gone to the superintendent's office to complain. The superintendent called a meeting with my principal, the library director, and some of the assistant superintendents for later that afternoon. I wasn't invited. I provided my principal with copies of the books I had, as well as information about the focus of the author visit. I was on my way home for the night when my principal called me on my cell phone to tell me the outcome of the meeting. The parent had filled out the appropriate paperwork in order to put *Glass* officially under review, and the author visit was canceled. I couldn't help but cry when she told me. I was so frustrated just knowing that the superintendent's cancellation of the author visit was a knee-jerk reaction made without much thought. I'm sure he hoped to avoid any bad press. Unfortunately, it didn't turn out that way.

In addition to feelings of anger, betrayal, and inadequacy, I had to figure out what to do about the author visit I had scheduled in exactly one week. There was no way I was going to cancel—I had to find an alternate location where Ellen could speak. After calling a friend and venting about the situation, she told me she would see about reserving the auditorium at the college where she teaches. It wasn't the best solution, because it would require my students to find their own transportation to the event, but it was better than nothing. The next day, after verifying the reservation for the new location, I e-mailed Ellen Hopkins to tell her what happened. I asked her if she was willing to speak at a different location and to a different audience. Luckily, she agreed.

It didn't take long for the story of the "uninvitation" to spread. Hopkins posted about it on her blog, and the story took off like wildfire on Facebook, Twitter, and censorship and news blogs.[1] By the time she arrived in Oklahoma City on Monday, September 21, newspaper articles were being planned.[2]

Because my author wasn't scheduled to speak until 7:00 p.m. on September 22, I took the opportunity to drive her to the local bookstores so she could autograph stock at Barnes and Noble, Borders, and Hastings. I made sure to pick up some additional books so people could purchase them after her presentation and get them autographed. Needless to say, her presentation was wonderful and enjoyed by all who attended. Unfortunately, there weren't many of my middle school students in the audience, but several teachers and librarians from my district were there to show support. Most frustrating, though, was the fact that only one school district representative came. The evening was a tremendous success, with approximately 150 people in attendance. The students that were there thoroughly enjoyed the opportunity to listen to Ellen Hopkins speak about her life, her writing, and her books.[3]

Probably one of the most frustrating elements of this controversy was when Kelly Ogle, a longtime television news personality in Oklahoma City, chose to feature the story on his short segment called "My 2 Cents." Ogle uses this segment to give his opinions about current issues around the state, the country, and the world. In his first mention of the book challenge, he stated that a parent sent him a list of excerpts from the book that contained inappropriate material.[4] This list included the number of times the f-word was used in the book. Ogle didn't stop there. A couple of days after his first segment, he recorded another one supporting his opinion that Ellen Hopkins's books weren't appropriate for middle school students and even went so far as to say they should be removed from the high school shelves.[5] This, even after he received a barrage of e-mails supporting Ellen Hopkins and her work.

My biggest complaint about the media coverage in general was the fact that everyone focused on the book challenge, which wasn't the problem. Yes, the parent challenged the book and filled out the official paperwork to take *Glass* through the reconsideration process, but that is the district's policy. The injustice was that Ellen Hopkins was not allowed to speak to the kids. It was a terrible decision.

I am in total support of parents submitting a request for reconsideration if there is a book they don't like in the library collection. They have the right to go through the process. What they don't have the right to do is dictate what other children can and can't read, or can and can't listen to in the case of an author visit. I was deeply offended with the outcome of this situation. I felt embarrassed, upset, disappointed, and unsupported by my principal and district. I had a huge chunk ripped out of my self-esteem and I feared I was going to hear "That librarian should be fired" fly out of someone's mouth at any minute. I was left questioning myself as a librarian and battling feelings of inadequacy. When I expressed these feelings to my principal, I was told that everyone gets "thrown under the bus" at some point in their career, and it was just my turn.

The reconsideration meeting was held on November 10, and I was able to attend as a nonvoting member along with my principal and an eighth-grade language arts teacher from my building. The parent who lodged the complaint was also invited to attend the meeting as a nonvoting member; she chose not to attend and not to provide a written statement to share her concerns about the book with the committee. The members of the committee with voting privileges were the district library director, the director of secondary education, the language arts coordinator, an assistant superintendent, an eighth-grade language arts teacher from another middle school, a middle school principal from another middle school, and a school board member. After everyone had a chance to speak about the book, the issue was called to a vote. It was determined that *Glass* would remain on the middle school library shelf. Although I was thrilled with the outcome, it made me angry all over again. There was absolutely no reason to have canceled Ellen Hopkins's author visit.

"By suppressing materials containing ideas or themes with which they do not agree, censors produce a sterile conformity and a lack of intellectual and emotional growth in students. Freedom in the public schools is central to the quality of what and how students learn," writes Henry Reichman.[6] That being said, what motivates people to attempt book censorship? Typically, Reichman summarizes, there are four main reasons:

Family values: A censor may feel threatened by changes in accepted and traditional ways of life.

Political views: A censor may view a work that is thought to advocate radical change as subversive or "un-American."

Religion: A censor may view explicit sexual works and politically or socially unorthodox ideas as attacks on religious faith.

Minority rights: Some censors want their own special group recognized. For example, ethnic minorities and women struggling against long-established stereotypes may want to reject materials that challenge their cause.

Basically, my censorship horror story originated from one parent's attempt to impose her family values on an entire eighth-grade population. Although she managed to get the author visit canceled, her attempt to remove the book from the shelf was unsuccessful, which seems funny to me since Hopkins's presentation was a lot tamer than the book's content.

NOTES

1. Ellen Hopkins, "Manifesto!!!!!" Ellen Hopkins: Yesterday, Today, and Tomorrow, entry posted September 17, 2009, http://ellenhopkins.livejournal.com/7107.html.

2. Jennifer Griswold, "Norman Parent's Questions Stop Author's Visit to School," News OK, September 22, 2009, http://newsok.com/norman-parents-questions-stop-authors-visit-to-school/article/3402996.

3. Jennifer Griswold, "After Norman Schools Snub, Author Ellen Hopkins Draws Crowd in Moore," NewsOK, September 23, 2009, http://newsok.com/after-norman-schools-

snub-author-ellen-hopkins-draws-crowd-in-moore/article/3403327; Julianna Parker Jones, "Controversial Author's Visit Continues Despite Cancellation: Books about Meth Addiction Draw Objection," Norman Transcript, September 24, 2009, http://normantranscript.com/local/x546384921/Controversial-authors-visit-continues-despite-cancellation.

4. News 9, "My 2 Cents: Norman Public Schools," CBS, September 2009, www.news9.com/Global/category.asp?C=116601&autoStart=true&topVideoCatNo=default&clipId=4154766&flvUri=&thirdpartymrssurl.

5. News 9, "My 2 Cents: Author's Book Still . . . ," CBS, September 2009, www.news9.com/Global/category.asp?C=116601&clipId=4167613&autostart=true.

6. Henry Reichman, *Censorship and Selection: Issues and Answers for Schools* (Chicago: American Library Association, 1993), 4.

CHAPTER 25

One of Those Not So Hideous Stories of a Book Challenge

KATHRYN PRESTIDGE

IT WAS the day before Thanksgiving break. Most of the staff had left the building shortly after the last bell, but theater rehearsal kept me at school until after 5:00. I returned to the media center to finish my day and make one phone call to a parent. Earlier in the day a parent had contacted the school's principal, concerned about a book in our school library. During my ten years as a media specialist in this small Wisconsin city, about a half dozen parents had voiced concerns about books in our library. From my experience as a public librarian, I knew that just listening to a parent's concern was the most effective approach.

I called the mother and we talked. She had picked up a book her daughter was reading from the school's library. The title drew her attention: *One of Those Hideous Books Where the Mother Dies* by Sonya Sones. Flipping through the book, one scene stopped her cold. Two teenage girls were discussing, what else: boys. One of the girls in the book states that, if you are still a virgin at fifteen, you are considered a loser. The voice on the phone paused as if expecting a shocked response from me. Instead, I used a nonthreatening communication technique called reflexive listening. I let her express her thoughts and responded by restating what I heard her say. Then I gave my usual careful explanation of the way I select books and strive to build a balanced collection. In this particular case, I explained that a well-read and articulate student had recommended this book to me. After checking reviews, I had purchased the book.

The concerned mother's daughter was an eleven-year-old sixth-grader—which may, in fact, be a bit young for this book; it is recommended for students in the seventh through twelfth grades. I affirmed this parent's right and responsibility to guide her own child's reading choices and offered to restrict those choices if I had a written request from her to do so. The tone shifted slightly, and she asked, "Do you feel *any* responsibility to these students?" Perhaps my voice tensed a bit as I carefully replied, "I feel the responsibility to offer them a diverse collection that will give them materials that they want to read." Finally, I explained the reconsideration procedure.

The reconsideration policy for our school district outlines a process for a citizen to follow who questions the appropriateness of library or classroom materials. It begins with a consultation with the building principal. If the citizen is not satisfied at that point, the concern is discussed with the superintendent. If the citizen wishes to proceed further, the curriculum director assists the citizen with filling out a formal request to convene the reconsideration committee. This group reads the book, discusses its characteristics, and makes a recommendation to the superintendent. The superintendent then makes the final decision. A provision for appeal to the school board is also included in the policy.

As our conversation came to an end, I gently encouraged the mother to read the entire book, saying I knew this author's characters usually ended by making wise moral decisions. Although obviously not satisfied, she indicated that she would not be pursuing the matter. After replacing the phone, I quickly typed a memo to my principal detailing the conversation, and I made a note to contact the Cooperative Center of Books for Children (CCBC) for information about this book. On the way home, I picked up a copy of the book to read.

A family crisis interrupted the enjoyment of my Thanksgiving break and swept everything about the book challenge from my mind. After the break, I contacted the CCBC to request book reviews and supporting materials. Then I was plunged into the final week of directing rehearsals and performances of the school play. Meanwhile, the crisis at home deepened and consumed my time away from school. Book challenges were not on my agenda.

Later, I received an e-mail from my principal informing me that the mother had decided to pursue her concerns and a meeting between them had been arranged. After unearthing an envelope in the bottom of my mail tray, I read her carefully written, polite letter. She stated that she had taken my advice to read the entire book, and though she thought it had the moral ending I had predicted, the path to that ending included too much inappropriate material. I saw that her complaint was addressed to the president of the school board with a copy sent to the superintendent. She had tried, unsuccessfully, to leapfrog the next step in the reconsideration process, which is a conference with the building principal.

I attended the meeting with the mother and the school's principal. The mother now had a stack of six more books in front of her: *What My Mother Doesn't Know* by Sonya Sones, the four books in the Sisterhood of the Traveling Pants series by Ann Brashares, and *Get Well Soon* by Julie Halpern. Obviously, she had been doing a little homework. In addition to her previous objections, she was concerned that the reading level of the first book was fourth grade though the content was obviously not appropriate for that age. There is a difference between reading levels and interest levels, I explained. A variety of both must be available to accommodate all types of students. My principal is a skilled reflective listener, and the tone of the meeting remained calm and respectful despite the subtle undertone of tension.

In the course of the conversation, I stated that I could put an alert on her daughter's library record. The alert is simply a pop-up note that appears on the computer screen whenever the patron's bar code is scanned. It could indicate any sort of reminder I wished to insert, from parental requests to damaged book notations. In the weeks to come, I regretted this statement many times and wished I had explained it more carefully. It was often misinterpreted by my administration and the public as an electronic filtering system, and it mushroomed into an imagined panacea for the problem of providing age-appropriate reading materials.

Although conceding the need to purchase a wide range of reading material, the mother left the meeting unsatisfied and determined to pursue the issue. I remained to continue the conversation with my school principal, a capable and caring man who had been suddenly thrust into the position of acting principal just a few months earlier. As I spoke to him about the need to find books that would reach out to all of our students and pull them into reading, my passion about this issue was released from the careful calm attitude I had maintained during the interview. When I said, "We have students who *live* what is in these books!" his expression changed and his patient look cleared. He had experienced an epiphany. He clearly understood what intellectual freedom meant for individual students. My spirits soared.

A blessing in disguise, my family concerns kept me from obsessing over this book challenge and the upcoming parent meeting with the superintendent. As I waited for results of the superintendent's private discussion with this parent, I asked myself what I would do if he told me to remove the book. Would I refuse to remove the book and jeopardize my job, or capitulate and just follow instructions?

Fortunately, the superintendent did not ask for the removal of the book. However, the parent decided to file a reconsideration request for the original Sones book plus the six other books. The superintendent and curriculum director determined that the titles would be reviewed one at a time by the reconsideration committee. All actions had been low-key to this point, but now, according to the school attorney, the open meetings law would go into effect and the press would become involved.

As required by the open meetings law, the superintendent's office submitted a notification of the meeting of the reconsideration committee to the local newspaper. The notice quietly appeared on an inside page. Eventually, the issue of a book challenge captured public attention and made the front-page news several times. Articles were printed in larger city newspapers, and video clips appeared on area television stations and on the Internet. Although the printed editorials usually reflected a restrictive viewpoint ("Traditional values are being contradicted by works of fiction in the school library"), the online blogs were overwhelmingly supportive of intellectual freedom ("Books kept me sane as a teenager").

In the meantime, I had received a wonderful packet from the CCBC's Intellectual Freedom Information Services, which included multiple book reviews, intellectual freedom articles, and the offer of further assistance if needed. I forwarded a copy of the packet to the superintendent for use during the reconsideration process.

The reconsideration committee (a standing committee comprising media specialists, a public librarian, community members, and school administrators) convened for the initial fact-finding meeting. Although open meetings laws allow the public to attend, only the mother, a newspaper reporter, one citizen, and I attended. The curriculum director explained the reconsideration procedure in detail. The mother spoke first, expanding on her written complaint but not belaboring her points. I read a short prepared statement about the book selection process. The meeting ended with a few questions from the committee members. Because no opinions or public comments were allowed at this meeting, it was short and "factual."

The next step was a public hearing, scheduled for the following month. At that meeting any community member could register to speak for three minutes. After much thought, I decided to approach the student who had first recommended the Sones book for our library. I asked if, with her parents' permission, she would be willing to speak at the hearing. Without hesitation she agreed. Not only did we obtain her parents' permission, but her father also registered to speak. Ten speakers and about twenty spectators, including a television cameraperson and reporter, attended the hearing—not quite the media frenzy the school's administration had feared.

Three people spoke in favor of removing the book. In addition, the author, Sonya Sones, had contacted the superintendent and submitted a supportive letter that was read at the hearing. One father, who apparently believed the so-called alert system was a form of filtering, stated that the use of the system would be adequate protection for his daughter without the removal of the book. The alert system was also cited as a solution by other speakers. Most supporters had not actually read the book but spoke on behalf of intellectual freedom. A science teacher simply talked about the positive role reading had played in surmounting issues in his own adolescence. The student who had recommended the book was ingenuous and direct: "This is a book about a girl whose mother dies. It shows how kids really are. Please do not take this book from our library."

When my turn came, I felt compelled to take a portion of my precious three minutes to carefully explain the "alert." I knew librarians everywhere were probably cursing me for causing people to think we had installed an automatic filter for age-appropriate books. No, I explained, the alert was nothing more than an electronic Post-it note, which would pop up whenever the student's bar code was entered. It was a simple system that had always been available in the form of any message attached to a student record. Hoping that I had clarified that point, I decided to ignore my prepared outline and speak from my heart: "I began working in my school library in seventh grade and have been a librarian in some capacity for almost forty years. My greatest joy is selecting books to entice students to read. To that end, I read hundreds of reviews and books, talk with colleagues, attend workshops, and listen to students. Middle school students are thinking about 'It' (sex), wondering about 'It,' and talking about 'It,' and I cannot just give them the Boxcar Children to read." And finally the sound bite that became my five seconds of fame: "In order to get these kids to read, I have to give them books which will speak to them and reflect their world."

The committee voted unanimously to recommend retaining the book, and the parent who had initiated the challenge left disappointed, but not defeated. She immediately appealed the decision to the school board. The appeal could not delve into the actual argument but could only be an appeal about proper procedure. During the appeal process, individual members of the school board could ask specific questions and raise other issues if they wished. During the appeal, the school board agreed that proper procedures had been followed and upheld the final decision of the superintendent.

One board member wished for clarification of the ubiquitous "alert system," and the president of the school board talked at length about holding a workshop meeting to explore the system fully. In the audience, I was sitting on my hands, screaming in my mind, "You don't need a workshop! There is no alert system. Just give me five minutes to explain!" No public comment was allowed, and I was powerless to stop the alert function run amuck. Nevertheless, the board voted to deny the appeal because the procedure had been meticulously followed.

Two subsequent challenges filed by the same parent resulted in recommendations to retain the books, and no other challenges or appeals have been filed as of this writing. Throughout the process, the district administration was supportive and assumed total responsibility for the challenge, never making it a personal event between the parent and me. In fact, I was often left to learn of meetings and appeals through hearsay and news articles. Although I chafed over the lack of direct communication with me, I appreciated the objectivity of the process designed to address citizen concerns.

This series of book challenges was actually my second brush with censorship. The first time I encountered censorship was in my Iowa hometown when the public librarians purchased a copy of *The Arrangement* by Elia Kazan and then returned it to the publisher with a scathing note about its unacceptable content. The publisher took the publicity opportunity and ran with it, even getting a spot on the Johnny Carson show to ridicule our small midwestern town.

In fact, the publisher gave free copies of the book to any citizen in the town upon request. There was no copy in my childhood home, however, because my father was on the library board and I was working in the library as a shelver. It was an interesting time and I learned to be wary of the media, which regularly skewed the facts. My father told me the library board had been advised not to respond to the press. They stuck to that resolve until the publicity faded and the incident was forgotten.

In time, I came to a deep appreciation of intellectual freedom and the right to read. I am still wary of the press, but the online comments made during my recent challenges helped me realize that there were more advocates of freedom of choice in our school district than I realized. During the reconsideration process, I decided to begin a library parent group, which gives parents a direct connection to the school library through parent/student book discussions, a wiki newsletter, and a venue for book purchasing suggestions. After the initial stab of apprehension when I knew I would be dealing with a formal book challenge, the reconsideration process became an opportunity for me to renew my appreciation of the democratic process, to articulate my own goals as a media specialist, and to improve parental communication in order to better serve my students.

PART VI

Crime and Punishment
When Library Patrons Have Committed a Crime

Instead of asking—"How much damage will the work in question bring about?" why not ask—"How much good? How much joy?"
—D. H. LAWRENCE

LIBRARIANS are expected to protect the privacy of every patron using a public library. The first chapter in this section involves a public library patron who is eventually convicted of a crime—but during the time he was using his community library, he was a patron with the rights, freedoms, and privacy protections afforded to all library users. The librarians in this chapter worked to provide law enforcement personnel with the information they needed while protecting the privacy rights of all other patrons using the library. In the second chapter some of the basic tenets of library work are challenged. Many security issues confronted by prison librarians challenge library ethics, and security demands may end access to books prisoners can read. The types of policies that protect librarians and their communities from censorship in public libraries are the same types of policies prison librarians employ to end unnecessary censorship.

CHAPTER 26

A Serial Killer Visits the Library

PAUL HAWKINS

ON FEBRUARY 25, 2005, Dennis Rader was stopped near his Park City, Kansas, home and taken into custody by law enforcement officials. Among the locations searched that day to obtain evidence in the infamous "Bind, Torture and Kill" (BTK) murders was the Park City Community Public Library.

Dennis Rader was a husband, father, former Scout leader, president of his Lutheran church congregation, Park City compliance supervisor, and local public library user. He was also the BTK killer. After his arrest, Rader detailed his torture and strangulation of seven women, one man, and two children during the period 1974–1991. For thirty years, the BTK killer had evaded and taunted law enforcement officials, sent messages about his crimes to local media, and terrorized the citizens of metropolitan Wichita, Kansas.

Dawn Pilcher, Park City Community Public Library director, remembers February 25, 2005: "The strangest and most bizarre day of my life. It's a memory that I will never completely forget, but it's also a memory that I don't relive often."

As director of the South Central Kansas Library System, I advised Pilcher during law enforcement officials' search of the library. Because of the sensationalism surrounding the BTK story and continuing issues regarding confidentiality, neither Pilcher nor I have commented publicly about the events. Now that several years have passed since Rader's arrest and conviction, we share our experience in the hope that it may prove valuable to others in the library community. Additional information in this chapter about the BTK murder investigations derives from various books and newspaper articles about the crimes.

"When you pull into the parking lot and see several police cars, you know something is going on and that it's serious," said Pilcher. A few minutes earlier, a team of officers from the Wichita Police Department and Kansas Bureau of Investigation pulled Rader over as he drove home for lunch. Rader surrendered without resistance.

According to Pilcher, "When I walked into the library, I was overwhelmed by the number of officers there. Some were in uniform and some in plain clothes and they all looked like they had revolvers. One of them showed me his identification and then they checked my ID. They showed me a copy of the search warrant and I read it immediately. They asked me to identify what each computer was used for and they also checked to see if a patron with the name 'Dennis Rader' had a library card. At this point, I didn't recognize the name 'Dennis Rader.'"

When the law enforcement officials had met the standards of proper identification and provided a legal search warrant, Pilcher complied with their requests. Unlike a subpoena to appear in court, the search warrant was immediately executable when Pilcher was served with it. The officers directed her to close the library until further notice and to not reveal any details of their investigation to the public. During the next five hours, Pilcher cooperated with the search but tried to make sure that only the records identified in the warrant were produced and no other records were viewed or copied. Borrower registration records indicated that Rader had a library card, but officers did not request to know what library materials he had checked out. Pilcher said investigators were more interested in examining the public access computer workstations.

"My main concern was that I comply with the law, assist as needed, but not compromise anyone's confidentiality," Pilcher said.

BTK murder investigations and Rader's confession reveal that the serial killer used the public libraries in Wichita and Park City. In 1974, the earliest letter from BTK was left at the Wichita Public Library, and thirty years later, in 2004, staff at the Wichita Public Library discovered another BTK communication in the book drop. Then, in February 2005, a floppy disk used by Rader at the Park City Community Public Library became the key clue in his identification as the killer. According to various sources, Rader had always used print as the means to communicate about his crimes with law enforcement and local media. But in 2004 he began digitizing and storing drawings, pictures, and writings about his murders in electronic formats. Rader had access to computer resources at his residence, city hall workplace, church where he was congregation leader, and the public library a few blocks from his home. One source cites the public library as the place where Rader "often did much of his research for his final barrage of communiqués to police."

On February 17, 2005, Wichita detectives received a new communication from BTK that included a purple 1.44 MB floppy disk. Immediately, a forensic specialist loaded the disk into a computer, clicked into the "prop-erties" field, and read the name "Dennis." In addition, metadata indicated that the disk was registered to Christ Lutheran Church and had last been used at the Park City Community Public Library.

Accounts of the investigation describe a simple Google search of "Christ Lutheran Church" that resulted in the first connection between serial killer BTK and new suspect Dennis Rader. Rader was listed as presi-dent of the church congregation.

Police immediately began surveillance of Rader, and they were later able to match DNA evidence to him. Rader eventually admitted guilt and was sentenced to ten counts of first-degree murder. Pilcher was never called to testify, and evidence obtained at the library was never presented in court. On August 18, 2005, Rader was sentenced to a minimum of 175 years without chance of parole and is currently incarcerated at the El Do-rado Kansas Correctional Facility.

During the five-hour closing and search of the Park City Community Public Library in conjunction with Rader's arrest, Dawn Pilcher and I were able to communicate using our cell phones. Given the directive by one of the investigators not to discuss any of the details of the situation, Pilcher felt constrained from talking. Nevertheless, she called me using her cell phone and, when I offered to advise her on-site, she indicated that law enforcement officials would not allow me to enter the library.

Early in her phone call Pilcher confirmed my intuition that the Park City Community Public Library had become part of the BTK murder in-vestigation. Having recently read a newspaper article about the discovery of BTK evidence in the Park City area, I correctly guessed that Park City Community Public Library had become more than the community's re-source for books, computers, and programs. Pilcher and I modeled our phone talk after a typical library reference interview in which I asked gen-eral questions that allowed Pilcher to provide mostly "yes" or "no" answers.

Because I was a consultant to our member libraries on how to handle law enforcement inquiries and Pilcher had participated in previous train-ing on the topic, we were fortunate to have the necessary background to frame our communications in a manner that allowed Pilcher to affirm or deny my questions and for me to elaborate and advise her on the basis of limited responses. If Pilcher had the opportunity to contact an attorney for advice, her communications would have fallen under attorney-client privilege, which would have made them confidential and not subject to constraint by law enforcement officials.

"Paul's reassuring me that the officers had correct documentation and other professional advice was helpful. He was encouraging and coached me on responses to law enforcement officials and the media," said Pilcher.

As news spread of the arrest of a suspect in the BTK murders, local media and sightseers began converging on Park City. Two helicopters could be seen overhead, and a local television station truck set up for a live broadcast directly in front of the library. A reporter and cameraperson were turned away from the library, and Pilcher refused a request for an interview.

"My standard reply was yes, the library was part of the BTK investigation and no, I can't discuss it," remembers Pilcher.

In the days following Rader's arrest and public awareness of his connection with the library, Pilcher continued to uphold user confidentiality. "We had policies in place regarding confidentiality, but the events caused us to reexamine and create new ones, especially in regard to media relations."

Pilcher did everything right when law enforcement officials closed the Park City Community Public Library to execute a search warrant in the BTK murder investigations. Fortunately, she valued and understood the importance of patron confidentiality. She had the training and support from the South Central Kansas Library System to address inquiries by law enforcement competently. Her library protected users' privacy by having the appropriate policies covering print and electronic records.

In hindsight, if officers had not already presented the search warrant and the investigation been in process, I would have advised Pilcher to have legal counsel review the document. The advice of an attorney provides a library with the highest degree of protection available. Still, on the basis of our discussion during the investigation, I felt reasonably assured that the search conformed to the terms of the search warrant. Nevertheless, it is such strict adherence to policy and procedure that must be expected even when a local suspect has just been arrested in a thirty-year serial killer investigation, an armed law enforcement presence has closed your library, two helicopters are droning overhead, and a media circus is assembled in the parking lot.

I commend the Park City Community Public Library director for her professionalism and courage. Under the dramatic and stressful circumstances surrounding the arrest of a suspected serial killer, she didn't fall apart or compromise library ethics. Although the library had only recently been established, its board of directors deserves credit for having adopted appropriate confidentiality policies. At our best, the library community trains and strives to uphold the values of confidentiality and intellectual freedom, but those ideals will be necessarily challenged in criminal investigations of serial killers such as BTK.

CHAPTER 27

Books, Bars, and Behavior
Censorship in Correctional Libraries

ERICA MACCREAIGH

Such as are thy habitual thoughts, such also will be the character of thy soul—for the soul is dyed by the thoughts.
—MARCUS ANTONIUS

Thought is action in rehearsal.
—SIGMUND FREUD

Even now, of course, there's no reason or excuse for committing thought crime. It's merely a question of self-discipline, reality-control.
—GEORGE ORWELL

CONTROLLING HUMAN thought has long been lauded—and vilified—as a means of controlling human behavior. Nowhere is this more evident than in jails and prisons, which, by their very nature, are designed to manage human beings. Censorship falls neatly within this function.

In correctional facilities, as in life, an uneasy tension exists between individual choice and the community's collective needs for safety, stability, and limited resources. Individuals find themselves behind bars when their actions disrupt this balance, when pursuing their own interests harms another and, by extension, society. The biographies of prisoners make it easy to argue that "garbage in" means "garbage out," and that "garbage" entails an immediate and compelling threat. From here, the slippery slope separating individual choice and social control comes into plain view.

In work environments and living communities built on exclusion, restriction, and surveillance, correctional librarians are often the lone champions of intellectual freedom. Armed, at most, with professional ethics, a solid collection development policy, the American Library Association's

Library Bill of Rights, and one of its newest interpretations, the Prisoners' Right to Read, correctional librarians bear the responsibility of defending offenders' access to all information, except when legitimate penological interests mandate exclusion.

The problem correctional librarians regularly face is broad interpretation of the definition of "legitimate penological interests." This term is widely used in legal literature to describe the goals and objectives of correctional institutions; some universal goals are confinement, staff safety, and rehabilitation. As correctional staff struggle to keep one step ahead of their charges, one offender's behavior problem frequently inspires facility- or department-wide changes to policy and procedure. Consequently, correctional facilities epitomize the concept of "managing to the exception." Wherever "legitimate penological interest" can be demonstrated, just about any action limiting everyone's access to resources and services is easily justified. The question rather infrequently asked is, Will this change in policy or practice resolve the problem at hand? The censorship translation of this question becomes, Will prohibiting offender access to certain material make the facility a safer place to live and work?

The short answer is "absolutely." But "absolutely" applies only in very singular instances. For example, correctional libraries don't tend to stock titles on the fine arts of lock picking, bomb manufacture, or home brewing with ingredients conveniently acquired in the dining hall. In reality, most challenges to correctional library materials fall within a vast gray area of interpretation and professional soul-searching as librarians align the Library Bill of Rights with the human right to safety of life and limb.

One of the most common pitfalls in correctional librarianship is confusing the content of a book with the intent of a prisoner. A schematic diagram describing how to disable the facility's security system or Grandma's recipe for sour mash—in other words, material describing functions obviously contrary to the goals of safety and security—is easy to prohibit. But what about the offender who requests a bus route map of the state's largest metro area? A reasonable assumption about why the offender is requesting this material might be that he wants to learn the area to figure out transportation from home to work after release. Upon discovering that the library has provided this information, however, administration immediately orders the librarian to remove all maps—including maps of the medieval spice trade, Tolkien's Middle Earth, and a globe. The administrator's assumption—and fear—is that the offender is planning an escape.

Try this one: an offender checks out a copy of *Parents Magazine*. One might assume he's keeping up with the developmental needs of his small children. The prison's administration, however, demands immediate suspension of the library's subscription. Why? The offender in question is a convicted pedophile. The fear is that nonadherence to his mental health plan puts children at risk.

How about this one: an offender is caught with several pieces of hand-drawn lined paper. One might assume he wants to write something neatly and legibly and can't afford notebook paper through the facility canteen. The prison administration demands that the library remove the sports pages from all newspapers. Why? There is a suspicion that the lined pages are for placing bets, the offender is running a gambling ring, and he's using the weekly statistics to set book. The fear is that the offender collecting debts is enjoying a dangerous degree of authority over other offenders.

Are these problems with public transportation, Gerber baby food ads, or the latest NFL rankings? Is this a failure of the library's collection development policies? Or is this a failure of individuals to follow the rules with a concurrent failure of the organization to deal directly with the individuals in question?

In corrections, failing to deal with individual behavior can have profound consequences. I am reminded of a passionate challenge to Laurell K. Hamilton's *Narcissus in Chains,* brought to my attention by a mental health physician who specializes in sex offender treatment. The book should be removed, the doctor said, because "it feeds offenders' violent sexual fantasies."

As a jail librarian by training and prison libraries consultant/supervisor by trade, I've been "behind bars" for several years and wasn't particularly surprised by the challenge. The title in question is typical of many recent offerings in the vampire genre—liberally peppered with hot sex and graphic violence (the same can be said of considerable mainstream fiction and most prime-time television, but this is not a very strong argument in a censorship dispute). In a prison dedicated to ambitious rehabilitative sex offender treatment, the library's provision of these types of books was perhaps understandably called into question.

Even in prison, most challenges to library materials, if properly handled at the point of complaint, don't progress to formal reconsideration proceedings. With this in mind, the facility librarian conversed at length with the doctor. She listened to his concerns about the book's subject matter and its potential impact on the inmate population. She explained the library's selection policies—mutually agreed upon by the State Library and the Department of Corrections—and asked the doctor if there was anything he'd like to see added to the library's collection to counterbalance Hamilton's subject matter. This generally reliable technique of discussing the material proved unsuccessful, so the librarian moved on to step two of the materials reconsideration policy and handed the doctor a formal reconsideration request.

As often as a sincere heart-to-heart conversation derails challenges to library materials, so too does the prospect of a formal reconsideration process. Put more simply, many challengers drop their complaint when they realize that paperwork is involved. The doctor's concern about his prison's sex offender community was sufficiently motivating that he did complete the paperwork, which, per policy, the facility librarian forwarded to me.

First a few words about dealing with challenges to library materials. Procedural escalation helps ensure that the challenge is addressed at the lowest possible level. Prison wardens simply don't need to be involved in every decision about the appropriateness of library materials. A good solid collection development policy outlining what the library will and will not stock, accompanied by a formalized multistep reconsideration process, keeps upper management out of most disputes and preserves the librarian's authority over the collection.

It is also mission critical to maintain emotional neutrality in a challenge situation; procedural escalation pales in comparison to interpersonal escalation. Visceral feelings overwhelmingly drive complainants and are generally triggered not by content, but by an idea. This returns us to the fundamental goal of most censors: controlling behavior by controlling thought. To a certain extent, they are right about the influence of one over the other, but even in a prison the censor exercises flawed logic when assuming that everybody needs to be protected from specific material.

When I received the doctor's formal complaint, I immediately saw problems that would require further discussion with him—namely, it wasn't clear exactly what the problem was with the book. To the question "To what aspect of the materials do you object?" he'd responded, "violent sexual content." To the question "Why do you believe this material is inappropriate for the general library collection?" he'd replied, "sex offenders in facility." My biggest challenge was his response to the question "Are there any desirable features about the material?" He replied, "Have not read it."

I couldn't do much with such sparse information, so I called the doctor. I began by thanking him for his interest in the library's collection and his concern for the offender population, and I recapped what I knew about his conversations with the facility librarian. Then I explained (again) the library's selection criteria, emphasizing that we look for specific content, not concepts, in making our decisions.

"But these books are filled with sex and violence! They're not even written well," he argued.

I explained that, regrettably, our selection criteria don't protect us from poor taste or bad writing. "What they [the policies] are intended to do," I ventured, "is prevent material from entering the facility that instructs or advocates dangerous and illegal activities. Just mentioning such things doesn't count. I'm looking for instructional material, for promotional material."

"I'm sure if you just open the book and read a few pages," he said, "you'll see what I'm referring to."

"I'm not sure of that at all," I replied. "You and I are different readers; we've got different personalities and probably some different values. I could read this book cover to cover and not see what you're seeing. In order to move forward on this in a productive way, I need you to tell me exactly what to look for."

He reiterated that he hadn't actually read the book, nor did he intend to. I assured him that I understood but explained again that I needed page numbers, quotes, and anything specifically pointing to content that might prohibit the material from staying in the library.

"I just don't think material that contains these kinds of pervasive sexual images and violence has any business in the hands of sex offenders," he grumbled. "Most of them in here aren't even allowed to have this material anyway."

"I'm sure that's true," I said. "And every one of them knows the requirements of his own mental health plan. Isn't it preferable, instead of sterilizing the prison environment beyond any semblance of the reality they'll face upon release, to instead provide some opportunities for them to exercise good choices for themselves? Wouldn't you rather know that one of your patients is struggling while he's here than discover after he's released that he still doesn't have what he needs to stop victimizing others?"

"Well," the doctor said, after a pause, "it *was* one of my patients who brought this book to my attention. He said it was feeding his violent sexual fantasies and he wanted me to take it away from him."

I said, "I don't think he needs you to take it away from him; he's demonstrating that he already knows what he needs to avoid. I see a win-win here. He's had the opportunity to sample a little of what the world is going to tempt him with, and he practiced responding appropriately. The next time he's tempted, it may be that much easier for him to do the right thing. I also see this as a very popular fiction series that is getting reluctant readers excited about books. Not every offender in this facility has the same problem as your patient. The library belongs to everybody. In this situation, that one book is serving two very different, very constructive purposes. If an offender is checking out materials he's not supposed to have, and those materials meet your library's selection criteria, the problem is with the offender, not with the library material. The offender's behavior in a safe, controlled environment can be monitored and dealt with. This is what 'corrections' is all about."

After just a few more minutes of discussion on this point, the doctor dropped his challenge, and I phoned the facility librarian to put the book back on the shelf.

Incarcerated offenders are encouraged to examine maladaptive thinking patterns that result in the kinds of antisocial behaviors that landed them in prison. Libraries provide opportunities for offenders not only to research material that can help them improve their lives but to exercise cognitive "muscles" like discretion and impulse control. The difference between an offender retraining his own thinking toward the goal of rehabilitation and correctional staff determining what is and is not acceptable subject matter is a gulf every bit as wide on the inside as it is on the outside.

The high road for librarians is also the same. I close with a quote from ALA's Prisoners' Right to Read: An Interpretation of the Library Bill of Rights: "The denial of the right to read, to write, and to think—to intellectual freedom—diminishes the human spirit of those segregated from society. Those who cherish their full freedom and rights should work to guarantee that the right to intellectual freedom is extended to all incarcerated individuals."[1]

NOTE

1. American Library Association, "Prisoners' Right to Read: An Interpretation of the Library Bill of Rights," www.ala.org/ala/issuesadvocacy/intfreedom/librarybill/interpretations/prisonersrightoread.cfm.

PART VII

Perhaps It *Is* Possible to Judge a Book by Its Cover

Displays

I believe in censorship. I made a fortune out of it.
—MAE WEST

DISPLAYS take books off crowded (sometimes even dusty) shelves and highlight special collections or special subjects. Library staff members create these displays with the hope that patrons will find new interests and inspiration. When displays are successful they can increase circulation, generate a lot of attention, and inspire thoughtful conversation. The attention displays create, when they are viewed by the diverse community that most libraries serve, also has the ability to create controversy.

CHAPTER 28

The Ghost of Halloween Past

KATHY BARCO

I'M STILL haunted by a near-challenge that involved *The Halloween Handbook* by Bridie Clark and Ashley Dodd. In our library, we routinely display books themed for upcoming holidays in a particular area of the children's room. One evening in early October, a parent found *The Halloween Handbook* on the holiday display. Descriptive phrases on the cover include "Dress-Up for Grown-Ups" and "447 Costumes." She brought it to one of the staff librarians and said it contained "inappropriate" costumes and we shouldn't have it in the children's area.

She particularly objected to a photo of a "genie" costume that consisted of opaque harem pants and a fairly high-necked top with three-quarter-length sleeves. The fact that the genie's bare midriff included an exposed navel was the offensive characteristic. The parent refused to complete a challenge form, saying, "No, I'm just pointing this out. You can take care of it." She was informed that the library could go no further with the complaint unless she filled out the form. She left without doing so.

The book, along with a short description of the incident, was put in the manager's office to be discussed the next day. The following morning, shortly after opening, the parent turned up in the library, looking for "that costume book." The manager brought it out and the parent began ranting that we shouldn't have that book in the children's area. At this point I had overheard enough to make me leave my post at the information desk in the children's room and step closer to overhear more of the discussion. The challenge procedure was outlined again, and the parent said she didn't want the book removed; instead, she wanted to check it out herself because there were some really great ideas in it. She then proceeded to point out her two favorites. First was the "chick magnet," which involved stapling/gluing/pinning leftover marshmallow chicks to a black shirt. That was followed by the "cereal killer," for which plastic knives are poked into miniature boxes of cereal, which are then attached to clothing. The parent checked out the book and left.

We never did hear what costumes she chose for her children. The book came back before Halloween and was displayed and checked out without incident. It has had good circulation, particularly when schools are holding "come dressed as your favorite character in a book" events.

CHAPTER 29

The Neophyte in the New Age

ROSEMARY J. KILBRIDGE

IT WAS an ordinary day in the summer of 1991 when one of the staff librarians put up a display in the case in the library's main reading room titled "Are You in the New Age? Discover It Here." The display consisted entirely of several books from the library's adult collection. All but one title relating to this multifaceted subject were particular to one of its aspects: yoga, astrology, the occult, and alternative medicine. The remaining title, which questioned the tenets of the New Age movement, was *Straight Answers on the New Age* by Bob Larson. This book was specifically mentioned by persons who subsequently objected to the display. I do not believe that the librarian deliberately mounted a one-sided display; we simply had a lot more material speaking to the attractions of the New Age than we did addressing its potential dangers.

As the director, I reacted favorably to the display, which was attractive. A week after the exhibit went up, letters started arriving in the mail. Six letters, dated August 6 through August 14, were spaced so that I received about one per day. All of the letters objected to the New Age display on the grounds that it proselytized a religion and was, therefore, in violation of the library's written policy on display spaces in the building.

The policy read, in part: "Religious or political displays may be constructed only if the topics are treated with no evidence of proselytism."

The letters, polite and well written, emphasized six main points:

The library has a right to have these books in the collection, and other people have a right to read them.

The New Age movement is a religious cult and the books are displayed in such a manner that the library appears to be endorsing this cult.

Parents are concerned that their children or other adults will become involved with the occult.

One book on the display questions the tenets of the New Age movement; the library should purchase more of these books.

People are angered that tax dollars are being spent to support this display.

The New Age movement has many controversial aspects.

Additionally, more than one writer mentioned having had personal negative experiences with a New Age group. Another writer asked if library displays were created by individual librarians or by a committee. Initially, I was completely baffled by the nature of the complaints and the relationship of religion to the New Age movement. I had considered the movement's elements part of a by-then-accepted lifestyle and societal shift; to me, it was a pretty "safe subject." As it happened, Wednesday, August 14, was the date of our regularly scheduled monthly board of trustees meeting. On that day, the meeting convened with the library director, the library's business manager, six of the seven trustees, and nine members of the general public in attendance. The absent trustee was, in fact, a practicing minister who happened to be out of town. Call it a combination of a tight time frame, a desire to avoid negative publicity, and the hope that this would somehow resolve itself easily, quickly, and quietly—but up to this point, I had not shared the content of the letters with the library trustees.

Several of the people who had written letters spoke during the meeting, repeating their written objections to the display—mainly, that the New Age movement was a religion, which the nature of the display encouraged or proselytized. The board discussed the matter briefly. Most of them seemed as perplexed as I by the nature of the objections; they too were unsure what the connection was with religion. There was no discussion of reasons why the New Age movement might be construed as a religion. The complainants themselves skirted the issue, which I later deduced was at the heart of the objection—mainly, that some proponents of the New Age movement practiced satanism.

This frustrating exchange during the board meeting boiled down to a request by those in the group to change the wording of the display to make it less compelling. The group requested that, if the board was not willing to amend the wording on the spot, a special board meeting should be held to decide whether the board was, in fact, violating its own policy by promoting the religious tenets of the New Age movement. I stated that I would not amend the wording without a clear directive from the board, which could not be voted on in the meeting because the item had not appeared on the posted agenda prior to the meeting. To allow for a forum for further discussion and to glean more insight into the specific nature of the request, the board directed me to do some research on the New Age movement and to schedule a special meeting to be held as soon as possible in order to make a decision about the issue. I could not help but feel that the group had initially pressed for another meeting in hopes that the missing minister would thence be present, presumably to support their cause. Upon learning that he would be back in town by August 20, I scheduled a meeting for that date.

The intervening week proved to be a hectic one. The city attorney and I reviewed our written "public display areas, bulletin boards and pamphlet racks" policy; fortunately, we had one. We could find no fault with the way the policy was written. The attorney opined that the complainants were confusing promoting an idea with providing information about an idea. He stated that we were not violating our policy. This situation occurred before we had Internet access, so I spent many hours conducting literature searches, scanning what books I could find, and delivering bulky packages of photocopied information directly to the trustees' homes. Contained in those packages was information I wish I had known when I first started receiving the letters of concern.

Although I was generally familiar with many of the components of the New Age movement, I had thought of it as mainly a presentation of alternative lifestyles and not as a religion. "New Age movement" is itself a controversial term applied to a very broad range of interests encompassing philosophy, mysticism, health, psychology, ecology, and the occult. The New Age is, of course, not new at all but the resurgence of the ever-present resistance to conformity with society's established order by various elements. The more secular aspects of the movement, such as the practice of yoga, the spread of alternative medical techniques, and the conservation activity of environmental protection groups, had been in the mainstream for years and were generally accepted to be positive societal changes. The spiritual components of the movement, however, were a different matter.

The spiritual aspects of New Age encompass not just neo-paganism, Wicca, and Hindu beliefs and practices but devil worship, or satanism. Knowing this, it is understandable that some Christians would view the New Age movement as directly in opposition to the teachings of Christianity. Christians could see New Age as a specific threat to their beliefs; hence, the labeling of the New Age movement a religion. The movement had risen to prominence in the United States most recently in the 1960s and 1970s, with many enthusiasts' identification with the "hippie" movement and the dawning of the "Age of Aquarius."

During my week of New Age research, a small flyer titled *Breaking the Evil Spell: Knocking the Creationists, Religious Fanatics, and Various Right-Wingers* was tacked to the library's lobby bulletin board. To this day I do not know whether this was coincidental or if someone else was silently commenting on the events unfolding inside the library. At this time, I also happened to mention the controversy to a friend who worked as a reporter for the local newspaper. Needless to say, a brief story appeared on the front page of the paper on August 18, two days before the scheduled special board meeting. The article was concise and factual and mentioned that the upcoming meeting was open to the public.

The meeting was duly convened at 4:35 p.m. on August 20, 1991. In addition to the full board, several members of the general public were in attendance, most of whom had been present at the initial meeting. After a brief summary of the events of the past two weeks by the board president, each trustee was invited to comment on the exhibit. Very little was said by the board members. Several citizens then voiced opinions, from which it was again apparent that those who spoke did not seek to remove materials from either the display or the collection but only to amend the wording on the display. In response to questions, I stated that I would make a concerted effort to achieve more balance in the collection by adding more materials questioning New Age beliefs.

After the discussion, the board voted unanimously (minister included) to leave the display contents intact but to change the wording on the display; I was left to decide what that wording would be. Immediately after the meeting, I removed the display lettering. The following morning I directed the librarian who had mounted the display to add the title "Books on the New Age," which she did.

I believe that the outcome was a positive one. We maintained the goodwill and the self-respect of the participants. We retained the display and the materials. I expanded the scope of New Age movement materials collected by the library. This was a challenging task, for I could not find much opposing material for a popular audience on the Age of Aquarius.

I had been caught completely off guard by the nature of this, my first serious censorship challenge. In reflecting back on this incident, and other challenges that we subsequently faced, I am struck by how deeply people hold their beliefs and how, when those beliefs are questioned, people are capable of showing a great deal of courage in standing up to what is, to many, an intimidating institution: the library board of trustees. This incident also suggests that people are reluctant to engage in frank discussions about religion in a public forum. It further raises the question of how well the public library, in general, serves the community's minorities.

What also struck me, repeatedly, was the amount of time and energy the entire process consumed. Over the years, I have been grateful that we did not have many formal challenges to materials, displays, or policies. At the time of this incident, the library board did have a written process in place for dealing with challenges. We have subsequently revised this procedure, partly as a result of receiving other challenges, not all of which turned out as well as this one. The formal process currently in place for dealing with challenges is time-consuming and involves several separate steps; in the heat of the moment and in the interest of time, all players become impatient with the process. In my recollection, we have had to follow the library's written procedure from start to finish only once.

Although the challenge described here was not the only one I faced during my career as a library director, it possessed the most interesting elements, received the most public attention, and resulted in one of the most satisfying resolutions.

CHAPTER 30

Gay Books Display Brings Out High School Faculty Prejudice

NADEAN MEYER

IT STARTED simply enough in spring 2005. As one of their assigned tasks, all our high school student library assistants were required to select and make a book display. They receive grades for their work in the library as vocational credit. "Andrea," a junior, decided in May to prepare a display of GLBTQ materials. She had seen a note somewhere that June is Gay Pride Month, and it resonated with her concern about fair treatment for all. I approved Andrea's topic and she gathered the material and made a book list and sign.

Our high school collection had many newer titles, *Luna, Boy Meets Boy, Empress of the World, Am I Blue? Geography Club, Rainbow Boys, My Heartbeat,* and classics such as *Annie on My Mind, Arizona Kid, Baby Be-Bop, Deliver Us from Evie,* and more. There were probably about twenty to thirty items in nonfiction and fiction. Andrea was pleased to see the choices and she quickly made a display. The next morning was the weekly teachers' meeting held in the library. It did not take long for comments from the staff to begin. I knew some of the teachers were conservative Christians and some were active members of Young Life for Youth, a Christian youth group, but I still did not anticipate the talk and the individual conferences that occurred in the next few days.

I had been the high school teacher-librarian for nine years and had gained credibility for my professionalism and teaching abilities. Some even understood how I valued the freedom to read based on the workshops, talks, and jointly prepared lessons at which I emphasized the importance of a variety of viewpoints in our materials. My previous principal strongly supported the library and my abilities to get students reading, but she had left three years earlier. The current principal was less sure of his authority, and he bent with the wind on many topics. Controversy in school libraries was not new to me.

The year of the challenge, I had been a librarian for thirty years and had experience teaching students about their freedom to read and my role as a librarian to provide them all types of materials. My first year as a public youth librarian resulted in a very public book challenge, but it taught me how to respond to book concerns. Over the years in elementary and high school libraries, I supported many books, films, speakers, and topics. I was comfortable with my ability to listen to parents, teachers, principals, and students who questioned why something was available in the library. I even taught courses in intellectual freedom and book censorship in two nearby universities for school administrators and school librarians.

Our high school of more than six hundred students is a small, semirural school near a larger town and university. We were one of the most diverse schools in the county, mainly because of the U.S. Air Force base within our boundaries; approximately one-quarter of our students were from the base.

I had been coadvisor of the Youth Suicide Prevention Team for more than seven years in our school, and I knew how some students who were gay or suspected of being gay were treated. I had learned that the library can be a refuge for some of these students during free time such as lunch. In the fall of the year of the GLBTQ display, our health teacher and counselor had arranged a facilitated session with selected staff and students (about 25 percent of the school) for community building. At this workshop, one of our high school seniors outed himself as gay and spoke of his harassment at school. Although the staff sometimes spoke about the incidents of particular students being bothered in the halls, we never discussed that information or consequences in any staff meeting.

A variety of faculty members met with me to oppose the display and ask for its removal that day:

The biology teacher had previously spoken with me about his objections to the Harry Potter books promoting witchcraft as a conservative Christian. Today he was angry but restrained. He told me the materials were un-Christian (based only on the display's sign) and inappropriate for our students. He went on to share that it would be the "last straw" for him if a student gay alliance formed at our school. I listened respectfully and answered quietly, telling him about the power of reading and learning about one's self and others. I told him about the Youth Suicide Prevention Team's work with students in our school, and how some students were treated when they were suspected of being homosexual. I thanked him for talking directly to me and listening to me.

The counselor was my coadvisor with the Youth Suicide Prevention Team and a longtime personal friend. We were neighbors even before I worked at the school. As an advisor for Young Life, she "felt this display was harmful and many faculty and students agreed with her," so she was telling me as a friend. She thought the display should be removed. Her statements were shocking to me. She knew how some students were treated. She said she counseled them on how to survive in this school, but she did not want to provide them with materials that could make our gay students trust themselves and their feelings. She did not want to provide our students with materials that could help these teens understand each other. The shock must have shown on my face as I reminded her of specific students who were currently suffering in school. I repeated my ethics and responsibility as a librarian to serve all students and said a curt good-bye.

The health teacher and I had worked together on a health grant for multimedia public announcements, so I knew she had conservative views. In my office she told me, "The display about homosexuality is not proper for high school because it makes this age student doubt their sexuality." She thought I was confusing questioning teens and that this age group should not be reading materials about homosexuality. I gently probed to see how she handled the topic in health class, and she said it was not discussed. I asked about the senior who had outed himself at her community-building workshop, and she said, "You know, he is in drama and was just looking for an audience." She shared that she has a lesbian sister and she, as a health teacher, believed that "it happened during her teen years by not being told what was correct." I was able to listen and thank her for talking directly with me, but I was flabbergasted by her opinion as a health teacher.

As a leader in the school, the head of the English department felt she needed to share with me that Andrea (the student who created the display) "was a troublemaker in one of the English classes." Andrea had brought up the topic of homosexuality several times in class that year and was "obviously looking for trouble." The English teacher thought it was unnecessary to point out that the school owned these books. For this objection, I found myself almost speechless, and so I reminded her that Andrea was completing an assignment for the graded library assistant class and that I felt she was doing it in an appropriate manner.

The next day I expected to find the principal at my door, but instead I was treated to the best gift—a complimentary education publication from the regional schools. Its fortuitous and timely arrival gave me new hope. The issue's cover story detailed how homosexuals were treated poorly in today's schools, particularly high schools. In this issue on treating all students fairly, many of my concerns were listed and verified with statistics and research. Upon finding this publication I stopped everything, sat down, read the article, shouted my excitement to our library assistant, and quickly made copies. I hand-delivered a copy of the article to our principal as I summarized the concerns from faculty. I told him of my intent for the display, that the topic choice was made by a student, and that students had learned about this topic throughout the year. I then phoned our assistant superintendent of curriculum, shared what was happening at the school, and provided him with a summary of the article. I talked until I heard him realize that the display was validated by the article.

I believe that it was the idea of fairness and use of statistics in our own regional schools that made a difference with my administrators' silent support. Whereas librarians understand the power of freedom to read, school officials often do not. Administrators are concerned about fairness and the data about students who drop out of school due to mistreatment. It is this approach and data that can drive the need for a wide range of material through school libraries.

We did not get a formal written complaint from any of the faculty or students in the school. In some ways I see that as a victory, but I also know that it was a sad indication to me of the climate of the school. Not one faculty member spoke to me in favor of the display. The faculty members who chose to talk to me directly were leaders in the school, and their opinions mattered. They held positions that directly affected our students: health, biology, counseling, and English. They had expected me to remove the display on the basis of their request and authority. The display remained until the end of school in mid-June.

As usual in high schools, talk about the display lasted only for a few days; then talk moved on to topics of graduation, finals, and state tournaments in sports. For Andrea, it was just one more assignment she completed and, at least this time, she had some choice about what to do. She was unaware of the faculty controversy that her display caused, but the feeling of distrust remained for me. Would these faculty members feel uncomfortable working with me in the future? Would our students share with each other that the library was a safe place to learn about all topics? Would the issue of fairness for all students ever be discussed by the faculty as a whole? I managed to speak my point of view, but it uncovered latent hostility directed at some of our students and the values of some of our staff. I know this discovery was part of my decision to leave this school one year later.

CHAPTER 31

Censorship Looms Over
the Rainbow

CINDY SIMERLINK

DURING GAY Pride Month a few years ago, I made a little display on a bookshelf end cap in the teen section. It included nonfiction and fiction books. Brent Hartinger and David Levithan were well represented in my collection at the time. (I was not able to have Alex Sanchez's *Rainbow Boys* or the sequels on the display because, despite reordering, our copies were always stolen. I always hope they're stolen by teens who want to own copies instead of censors who want to make them unavailable.) I had made a sign with a rainbow saying "Gay Pride Month" and a sheet with a bibliography of GLBTQ books available at my branch. An adult male came up and complained that we shouldn't be promoting such gay issues. The staff member brought the branch manager into the conversation to take over. The manager was polite but firm. She explained the library's policy of providing information from a variety of viewpoints, and that it was appropriate for the teen librarian (me) to choose to display these materials in the teen section.

An hour later a colleague noticed that the two sheets of paper—the sign and the bibliography—had been removed. I rolled my eyes and re-printed them. The next week I was on vacation, and when I came back I was told that the two signs had been removed again. I reprinted and reposted. I believe they were removed a third time, but it was at the very end of the month so I just changed the display.

In the years following that incident, the same man has complained several times about the magazine *Sex, Etc.* (One time he was objecting to the word *masturbation* on the cover where his six-year-old could see it. We managed to refrain from asking him how his six-year-old happened to be able to read and understand this word.) The magazine is displayed face-out in acrylic brochure-type holders on a bookshelf end cap in the teen section, just like the other teen magazines. (I believe he regularly browses the teen graphic novel section located there.) He has even called the downtown library and spoken to the director about removing the magazine, but he never fills out the reconsideration form so no action has been necessary. But I still grit my teeth when I see him walk into the library.

DISCUSSION QUESTIONS

Sometimes We're Our Own Worst Enemy: When Library Employees Are Censors

- What would you do if you had to defend material owned by your library that you found personally disgusting, disturbing, dangerous, or upsetting?
- How should library employees be trained about the importance of First Amendment issues? When should this training occur?
- What wording in a collection development policy might lend support to librarians who must select controversial material as part of their responsibility to the library community?
- Should library employees be terminated when they censor material?
- How would you prove that a library employee intentionally engaged in censorship? Does your library have a policy for working with employees who are accused of censorship?
- Several forms of book censorship are described throughout this book: books thrown in trash cans; items made to disappear by a disgruntled critic who fails to remove them via the official channel; material removed by library employees who don't want to chance further challenges; and items spirited away by young patrons who are too embarrassed to check them out. Do you have any experience dealing with these forms of censorship? If so, describe your experience.
- How should library policies address staff concerns regarding the acquisition and availability of library materials? Do your library's collection development and materials reconsideration policies address the responsibilities of library staff members?

How Dare You Recommend This Book to a Child: Reading Levels and Sophisticated Topics

- How should a library determine where to place a book? How does your library decide if a book belongs in the adult or children's section of the library?
- As described throughout this book, libraries have different ways of helping parents when their minor child is checking out material. What policies and procedures should libraries have in place regarding children and the items they check out?
- How does placing books in alternative sections, recataloging books, or creating special collections for certain types of books impact library users? Does changing the location of an item allow for more use or less use?

- Should it be the responsibility of a library to develop or use a rating system for books, music, films, or games? What are some of the pros and cons of developing or using a rating system?
- Should parents be able to monitor the library accounts of their minor children? Why or why not?
- Where should graphic novels be housed in a library? Should they be within a larger collection, or should they be segregated as a separate collection? What are the pros and cons of each decision?
- What laws exist in your community in regard to librarians acting in loco parentis? Are librarians who attempt to restrict children from checking out material opening themselves up to lawsuits in your community?

Not Only Boy Scouts Should Be Prepared: Building Strong Policies

- What are the most important elements to include in a collection development policy?
- How much input should patrons have on collection development? What are the pros and cons of having a collection development committee?
- Can your library defend a decision not to purchase specific library material?
- What questions and statements should be included on a materials reconsideration form?
- Many materials reconsideration forms require that the challenger read the entire book. Why should or shouldn't this be a requirement for submitting a form for reconsidering library material?
- In his chapter 2, James LaRue writes that by making the filling out of a reconsideration form the patron's last step in the challenge event, the number of written challenges his library receives has been greatly reduced. This strategy requires that staff members actively engage patrons, listen to their complaint, and ultimately bring in a supervisor if resolution isn't reached. Would you or your staff be comfortable with this procedure?
- Several chapters in this book discuss children's books with "hot button" gay-themed stories that had been challenged and retained but were ultimately weeded from the collection. Might you be disinclined to weed such titles, in an almost "reverse-censorship" move, in order to maintain or demonstrate the diversity of your holdings?

When the Tribe Has Spoken: Working with Native American Collections

- What should the librarian's role be in protecting culturally sensitive information?
- Should libraries and archives restrict access to culturally sensitive material?
- In the area of culturally sensitive material, should librarians ask patrons how they are going to use the material before permitting them access?
- Should librarians ever be responsible for "hiding" information?
- Should libraries holding Native American materials (or material concerning

Native American cultures) maintain a relationship with these cultural groups and follow their requests when it comes to removing or retaining information?

Conversation + Confrontation + Controversy = Combustion: Vocal Organization and Publicly Debated Challenges

- How should a library and its staff prepare for a book challenge launched by a national organization with political motives?
- How important is it to have established community relationships prior to a challenge to library material?
- While standing up to groups/people who want libraries to remove material from the collection, how should librarians react to personal attacks?
- Several chapters in this book recommend steps to take in the face of a challenge:

   Speak with one voice by allowing only one spokesperson.
   Emphasize the library's position on confidentiality.
   Spread the truth.
   Do not be drawn into the debate.

   Do any of these recommendations seem like they would be especially difficult to follow?
- How would your library enact these policies and activities?
- Given the experience Karin Perry describes about Ellen Hopkins's canceled visit, would you consider inviting a controversial author to speak at your library?

Crime and Punishment: When Library Patrons Have Committed a Crime

- In the account in chapter 26, a librarian was required to provide information to the FBI. Could your library's policies address issues that were brought out in that situation? Would every member of the staff know how to respond to a similar request for patron information at your library?
- In chapter 27, Erica MacCreaigh writes about the content of a book versus the intent of the patron. How does this type of thinking relate to book challenges in school, academic, and public libraries?

Perhaps It Is Possible to Judge a Book by Its Cover: Displays

- How are library displays different from the library's general collection? Is it necessary to have a policy about library displays?
- Is a display on any subject a library endorsement of that topic or point of view? Why or why not?
- In one narrative, the author mentions a controversy to a friend who worked as a reporter for a local newspaper. As the director of the library, she could choose to contact the media. Some libraries have policies prohibiting staff from talking to reporters. Does your institution have such a policy, and

can you imagine some circumstances under which you would be willing to ignore it?

- In chapter 29, a conflict was resolved by changing the name of a display: "Are You in the New Age? Discover It Here" became "Books on the New Age." The change allowed people viewing the display to know immediately what it was about. Similar to reading the label on packaged food or the "surgeon general's warning" on tobacco products, this makes the viewer a more informed consumer. Could this whole incident have been avoided if from the beginning there had been more detailed labeling of the display?

CONTRIBUTORS

Lucy Bellamy is currently the head librarian at her institution. Lucy earned her MLIS from San Jose State University's School of Library and Information Science. She received her BA in liberal studies with a minor in English literature and women's studies from California State University, Northridge. She is a member of ACRL, the Special Libraries Association, and California Academic and Research Libraries. Her professional interests include information literacy best practices, enhancing faculty-library collaboration, collection management, and developing copyright practices in the for-profit education setting.

Susanne Caro is the state documents librarian at the New Mexico State Library, where she tries to share her enthusiasm for the strange and wonderful subject of state documents. She attended the College of Santa Fe and earned a BA in creative writing. After working at Fogelson Library at the College of Santa Fe, she earned her MLS from Texas Woman's University in Denton.

Lisë Chlebanowski got her start in libraries in Downers Grove, Illinois. In 1994, while working part-time at the library and raising three children, she ventured back to school to finish the bachelor's degree she had abandoned twenty-five years before and then went on to complete her MLIS at Dominican University in River Forest, Illinois. A month after receiving her master's degree in 2003, she and her husband escaped to Arizona, choosing sunshine over snow. She has presented her program "How 'Sex' in the Library Changed My Career" at several State Library conferences. She has more than fifteen years' experience in libraries.

Lauren Christos graduated from the University of South Florida in 2000 and received the Distinguished Alumni Award. Christos works at Florida International University in Miami. She is past chair of both the Florida Library Association Intellectual Freedom Committee and the ALA Intellectual Freedom Round Table. In addition, she has held numerous positions within IFRT such as program chair, director, and editor of the *IFRT Report*. Christos is also active in local, state, and national civic engagement issues. Her other passions include Burning Man. She presented "Ephemera: Archiving and Preserving the Burning Man Experience" at the Popular Culture Conference in San Francisco.

Ron Critchfield has more than fifteen years as a professional librarian. He has been an assistant director of an academic library, a college professor, and a statewide library consultant for the Commonwealth of Kentucky. He is currently the executive director of the Jessamine County Public Library in

Nicholasville, Kentucky, and has a special interest in information literacy and intellectual freedom. Critchfield earned a PhD in information science from Nova Southeastern University, an MLS from the University of Kentucky, and an MTS from Duke University.

Amy Crump has served as the director of the Marshall Public Library in Missouri since 2004. She earn an MLS from the University of Illinois, Urbana-Champaign. Crump is a fledgling storyteller, relishes the works (both past and future) of Kristin Cashore, and loves a good librarian joke. At least one of their three children has threatened to become a librarian.

Sydne Dean is associate director of public services at the Pikes Peak Library District in Colorado. She has been employed by the library for thirty-one years and in charge of the library's materials reconsideration process for about twenty of those years. In 2003 she was awarded the Julie J. Boucher Intellectual Freedom Award by the Colorado Association of Libraries. Dean obtained her BS in education from the University of Pennsylvania and MLS from the University of Alabama.

Robert Farrell is the coordinator of information literacy and assessment at Lehman College, City University of New York. He holds an MLS from the University at Buffalo and an MA from the CUNY Graduate Center.

Natasha Forrester is a youth librarian with Multnomah County Library in Portland, Oregon, with a special interest in outreach to at-risk and immigrant families and parent/caregiver workshops on the importance of early literacy. She is a certified Every Child Ready to Read trainer, has presented at state and national conferences on topics such as working with teens and programming and early literacy work with English-language learners, and she is active on state and national library association committees.

Alisa C. Gonzalez is the reference coordinator and social sciences librarian at New Mexico State University in Las Cruces. She received her MLIS from Kent State University in Kent, Ohio. Gonzalez has been fortunate to have worked in both public and academic libraries throughout her professional career. Most of her experience with censorship has been in public libraries in Ohio and Texas. Her research interests include the cultural and sociological aspects of library use as well as graduate student information-seeking behavior.

Gretchen Gould is a reference librarian and bibliographer at the University of Northern Iowa. Her subject specialties as a librarian and bibliographer include government documents, maps, political science, law, geography, and military science. She received her MSLS from the University of Illinois at Urbana-Champaign and later a master's degree in history, with a thesis titled "Obscenity and Pornography: A Historical Look at the American Library Association, the Commission on Obscenity and Pornography (1970), and the Supreme Court."

Paul Hawkins is director of the South Central Kansas Library System, which provides grants, consulting, continuing education, and support to 147 member public, school, academic, and special libraries in twelve counties. During the past twenty-five years, Hawkins has advised member librarians and library boards on numerous confidentiality and intellectual freedom issues.

Hollis Helmeci is director at Rusk County Community Library in Ladysmith, Wisconsin, and has been director of Bradford Memorial Library in El Dorado, Kansas. Helmeci has worked in four states as a youth services librarian, a branch manager, and a public library director. She has a PhD in American literature and an MLS with an emphasis in youth services.

Gayle Hornaday received her MLS from the University of Illinois at Champaign-Urbana in 1977 and has been a public librarian for over thirty years. Her first library job was during college, typing catalog cards. Witnessing the integration of digital technology into library operations and services has been an exciting part of her career. She has worked as a reference librarian in Winnemucca, Nevada, and Findlay, Ohio, as well as in the Milwaukee area. Since 1994 she has been at the Henderson Libraries in Nevada, where she has been assistant director since 1996.

Peggy Kaney currently serves as the assistant dean of libraries at Northeastern State University in Tahlequah, Oklahoma. She is also pursuing a PhD in library and information management at Emporia State University. She has taught both children's and young adult literature courses for future teachers and librarians. Prior to her move to an academic library, she worked for thirteen years in youth services for the Tahlequah Public Library.

Rosemary J. Kilbridge is a recently retired librarian whose career spanned thirty-six years. Her experiences included organizing slides in a college art history collection in New York State, cataloging in a large university in New York State and in a medium-sized public library in Wisconsin, directing the activities of a small library in western Wisconsin, and reorganizing a high school library in rural South Africa. After nearly four decades of working full-time, she is catching up on sleeping and reading, in that order.

James LaRue has been the director of the Douglas County (Colorado) Libraries since 1990. He is the author of *The New Inquisition: Understanding and Managing Intellectual Freedom Challenges* (Libraries Unlimited, 2007) and has written a weekly newspaper column for over twenty years. He was the Colorado Librarian of the Year in 1998, the Castle Rock Chamber of Commerce's 2003 Business Person of the Year, and the winner of the 2007 Julie J. Boucher Award for Intellectual Freedom.

Erica MacCreaigh has worked in libraries for two decades, including twelve years in jail and prison libraries and public library outreach. As a correctional libraries senior consultant with the Colorado State Library, she oversees operations at nine Colorado state prison libraries serving nearly five thousand inmate patrons. MacCreaigh holds an MLIS from the University of Wisconsin-Milwaukee and regularly presents workshops on public library outreach and prisoner reentry. She coauthored *Library Services to the Incarcerated: Applying the Public Library Model in Correctional Facility*

Libraries (Libraries Unlimited, 2006) and coedited *On the Road with Out-reach: Mobile Library Services* (Libraries Unlimited, 2010).

Michelle Martinez is an assistant professor and reference librarian, as well as the English and literature bibliographer, at Sam Houston State University. Previously she was a public librarian. Martinez received an MA in English from Sam Houston and an MS in library science from the University of North Texas.

Theresa McDevitt is a librarian at Indiana University of Pennsylvania, where she has served as university archivist. She has a PhD in nineteenth-century American history and has written articles and a book on women in America. She is currently working on a history of women at Indiana University of Pennsylvania to coincide with the twenty-fifth anniversary of women's studies there.

Nadean Meyer is learning resources librarian at Eastern Washington University, where she oversees the curriculum center and works with education faculty and students across campus. She worked for twenty years in elementary and high schools as a school librarian and teacher of gifted students and multimedia production. She currently coteaches about intellectual freedom in the young adult literature class for reading majors. She belongs to the Freedom to Read Foundation as well as AASL, ACRL, ALSC, and YALSA.

Cathlene Myers Mattix grew up in Southern California and graduated from Oklahoma State University. She has lived and worked in human services in several states during her adult life and recently turned a hobby into a job when she became a genealogy librarian.

Matt Nojonen has been director of the Pataskala (Ohio) Public Library since 1995. He earned an MLS from the University of Missouri-Columbia in 1991. He has worked in large urban, suburban, and small rural libraries in various capacities since 1987. He considers himself fortunate to have worked with two great people: Brenda McDonald at the St. Louis Public Library and Renee Croft at the Holmes County Public Library.

Susan Patron served as the juvenile materials collection development manager for the Los Angeles Public Library from 1980 to 2007. She is the author of the Lucky's Hard Pan trilogy published by Atheneum Books for Young Readers.

Angela Paul received her teaching certificate and library endorsement at the University of Northern Iowa in 1991. Her first library position was at the American Institute of Business in Des Moines. She later became librarian at St. Katharine's St. Mark's College Preparatory School, a private K–12 school in Bettendorf, Iowa. While at Coleman Middle School, in Wichita, Kansas, she began MLS course work in Emporia, Kansas, and graduated in 2004. She is currently working as the instruction and outreach librarian at Wichita State University.

Kristin Pekoll has been young adult and reference librarian at the West Bend (Wisconsin) Community Memorial Library since 2002. She started out in the circulation departments of various libraries throughout high school and college while completing a BA in English and information technology and a MA in library science at the University of Wisconsin–Milwaukee. Pekoll has been passionate about intellectual freedom since her first information science class with Elizabeth Buchanan.

Karin Perry earned her bachelor's degree in elementary education in 1998. After working as a fifth-grade teacher for two years and finishing her MLIS from the University of Oklahoma, she became a school library media specialist at a small elementary school in Norman, Oklahoma. Four years later she moved to a middle school to act as school library media specialist for the next five years. Karin completed her PhD in July 2010 and took a position as assistant professor at Sam Houston State University in Huntsville, Texas, in 2011. She reviews young adult literature on her blog at www.karinsbook nook.com.

David M. Powell has held positions as an assistant reference associate, reference librarian, cataloger, and technical services manager. He is currently working at the Jessamine County Public Library in Nicholasville, Kentucky, as the circulation services manager and is in charge of the acquisition of graphic novels, music CDs, and DVDs. Powell has an MLIS with specialization in school media from the University of Kentucky.

Kathryn Prestidge began her library work in 1965 as a high school page in a small Iowa public library. She earned an MLS from the University of Iowa. Her career in libraries includes positions as children's librarian in a big city library, interlibrary loan/circulation clerk of a small college library, director of a very small public library, children's librarian of a small public library, and media specialist in a middle school library. She also engages in occasional storytelling and writing.

Cindy Simerlink has been a librarian since graduating from Florida State University in 1995. She has been a reference librarian, a medical librarian, a cataloger, and a teen librarian. She works at a large branch library in Huber Heights, Ohio, in the Dayton Metro Library System. She loves helping people, recommending books, and making a difference to teens, especially by showing them by example that it is okay to enjoy doing crafts even if your results look like a third-grader's.

Laurie Treat received an MLIS from the University of Southern Mississippi in 2006. She has worked with high school students for twelve years, as both a U.S. history teacher and a librarian. She currently is a member of ALA, AASL, YALSA, NEA, and the New Mexico Library Association, and she does committee work in Advocacy for School Libraries, a special interest group of the New Mexico Library Association. She has helped establish New Mexico Reads promotional materials for literacy sponsored by the New Mexico Library Association.

Marie-Elise Wheatwind is a teacher of high school and college English. She has master's degrees from U.C. Berkeley (English), the University of New

Mexico (education), and the University of Arizona (library science). Her teaching has garnered recognition and awards in New Mexico. Her writing has been awarded a PEN Syndicated Fiction Prize as well as literary grants from California and Oregon.

Sherry York worked as an educator from 1969 through 1999 in four Texas school districts. She holds an MA in education and is certified in supervision and mid-management and as a secondary teacher and all-level librarian. York has published articles and reviews in numerous journals. She is the author of *Picture Books by Latino Writers* (2002), *Children's and Young Adult Literature by Latino Writers* (2002), *Children's and Young Adult Literature by Native Americans* (2003), *Ethnic Book Awards: A Directory of Multicultural Literature* (2005), *Booktalking Authentic Multicultural Literature: Fiction, History, and Memoirs for Teens* (2008), and *Booktalking Authentic Multicultural Literature: Fiction and History for Young Readers* (2009), all from Linworth Publishing.

INDEX

You may also be interested in

Copyright Law for Librarians and Educators: Creative Strategies and Practical Solutions, Third Edition

KENNETH D. CREWS

Copyright in the world of digital information is changing at a fevered pace, even as educators and librarians digitize, upload, download, draw on databases, and incorporate materials into Web-based instruction. Crews has completely revised his classic text to remap the territory with fresh, timely insights into applications of copyright law for librarians, educators, and academics.

ISBN: 978-0-8389-1092-4
208 pages / 8.5" x 11"

INTELLECTUAL FREEDOM MANUAL, EIGHTH EDITION
OFFICE FOR INTELLECTUAL FREEDOM (OIF)
ISBN: 978-0-8389-3590-3

COMPLETE COPYRIGHT FOR K–12 LIBRARIANS AND EDUCATORS
CARRIE RUSSELL
ISBN: 978-0-8389-1083-2

COMPLETE COPYRIGHT: AN EVERYDAY GUIDE FOR LIBRARIANS
CARRIE RUSSELL
ISBN: 978-0-8389-3543-9

PROTECTING INTELLECTUAL FREEDOM IN YOUR PUBLIC LIBRARY
JUNE PINNELL-STEPHENS FOR OIF
ISBN: 978-0-8389-3583-5

PROTECTING INTELLECTUAL FREEDOM IN YOUR SCHOOL LIBRARY
PAT R. SCALES FOR OIF
ISBN: 978-0-8389-3581-1

PROTECTING INTELLECTUAL FREEDOM IN YOUR ACADEMIC LIBRARY
BARBARA M. JONES FOR OIF
ISBN: 978-0-8389-3580-4

Order today at **alastore.ala.org** or **866-746-7252!**
ALA Store purchases fund advocacy, awareness, and accreditation programs for library professionals worldwide.